Paul Vincent Carroll

THE IRISH WRITERS SERIES
James F. Carens, General Editor

PAUL VINCENT CARROLL

Paul A. Doyle

Lewisburg
BUCKNELL UNIVERSITY PRESS

Associated University Presses, Inc.
Cranbury, New Jersey 08512

ISBN: 0-8387-7764-3 (cloth)
      0-8387-7659-0 (paper)
Printed in the United States of America

Contents

Contents

Acknowledgments

I express deep and sincere appreciation for much information, help, and kindness to Miss A. J. Nancy Carroll, the playwright's sister, and to Kathleen and Helena Carroll, his daughters.

I also gratefully acknowledge the assistance, encouragement, and generosity of Professor Robert Hogan, whose Proscenium Press has been a boon to modern drama. I thank several diligent librarians at the Library of Congress and at The Theatre Collection of the Research Library of the Performing Arts at Lincoln Center. Further gratitude is extended to the Academic Center Library of the University of Texas and to the Manuscript Committee of the Academic Center Library.

Chronology

1900: July 10—Paul Vincent, the son of Michael and Kitty Sandys Carroll, born at Blackrock, near Dundalk, County Louth, Ireland.

1913–1916: Attended St. Mary's College, Dundalk, Ireland.

1916–1920: Attended St. Patrick's Training College, Dublin. Wrote short stories and poetry for *Ireland's Own* and for the *Irish Weekly Independent*.

1920: Returned to Dundalk but decided to take a teaching position in Scotland.

1921–1937: Taught in various state schools in Glasgow; spent considerable time writing plays. Also wrote many short stories and book reviews for Scottish newspapers. Continued to write occasional short stories for newspapers and magazines throughout his lifetime.

1923: Married Helena Reilly in Glasgow.

1930: *The Watched Pot,* Carroll's first produced play, presented at the Peacock Theatre, Dublin.

1932: Won an Abbey Theatre prize for *Things That*

Are Caesar's (originally called *The Bed of Procrustes*) first produced at the Abbey Theatre.

1933: Carroll and two friends founded a neighborhood theatre in Glasgow.

1934: *Things That Are Caesar's* first published.

1936: Received the Casement Award of the Irish Academy of Letters.

1937: *The Coggerers,* a one-act play, produced at the Abbey Theatre in November. *Shadow and Substance* first produced at the Abbey and published. Won the New York Drama Critics Circle award for the best foreign play of the 1937–1938 season. *Interlude* first published in the *Dublin Magazine.*

1939: *The White Steed* first produced at the Cort Theatre, New York City, and published. Won the New York Drama Critics Circle award for the best foreign play of the 1938–1939 season. *Kindred* produced. *Plays for My Children* published. Served as the "resident" playwright of a little theatre founded by Molly Urquhart at Rutherglen, Scotland. Gave several lectures on drama to various groups in the United States in 1939 and 1940. *Coggerers* published.

1940: *The Old Foolishness* produced. In the early 1940s continued to write book reviews and also wrote an anecdotal column called "Standing on the Corner" for Scottish newspapers.

1942: *The Strings, My Lord, Are False* produced.

1943: One of the founding directors of the Glasgow Citizens' Theatre.

1944: *The Old Foolishness* and *The Strings, My Lord, Are False* published in separate editions. *The Wise Have Not Spoken* produced at the Abbey Theatre. A revised version of *Things That Are Caesar's* published containing a completely new and, in Carroll's view, much stronger final act.

1945: Took up residence in England to be near the British film industry. For several years he wrote movie scenarios and later wrote for television. He continued for many years to serve both as an author of, and as an advisor on, movie and television productions. His most notable contribution to the cinema was an original story *Saints and Sinners* filmed (1949) under the aegis of Sir Alexander Korda. Bosley Crowther, the *New York Times* movie critic, noted that the story had "grand humor, tenderness and charm" and called it an "utterly beguiling little film."

1947: *The Wise Have Not Spoken* first published. *Green Cars Go East* published. *Interlude* published in a separate edition. *Conspirators* published (the title was originally *The Coggerers*). The following children's plays published in separate editions: *St. Francis and the Wolf; Beauty is Fled; Death Closes All; His Excellency, the Governor; The King Who Could Not Laugh; Maker of Roads.*

1948: *Weep for Tomorrow* produced and circulated in typescript form.

1950: *Chuckeyhead Story* produced. This play was

later called, with some revisions, *Border Be
Damned* (1951), and then, with further revisions, entitled *The Devil Came from Dublin*
(1951).

1951: *Green Cars Go East* produced.

1955: *The Wayward Saint* produced and published.

1956: *Farewell to Greatness* presented on BBC Television. *Goodbye to the Summer* (a revised version of *Weep for Tomorrow*) completed and
made available in typescript form.

1958: *Irish Stories and Plays* (includes the first pub-
lication of *The Devil Came from Dublin*—final
revised form of the text). This version differs
somewhat from the 1951 text. Several years later
Carroll collaborated with Bernard Wiesen on
as yet unproduced film version of *The Devil
Came from Dublin.*

1966: *Farewell to Greatness* first published.

1968: October 20—Carroll died suddenly at his home
in Bromley, Kent, a suburban area of London.
Carroll had been in poor health because of a
heart condition.

1970: *Goodbye to the Summer* first published.

Paul Vincent Carroll

I

Twentieth-century literary histories and reference works generally give only relatively brief space to Paul Vincent Carroll. His two most famous plays—*Shadow and Substance* and *The White Steed*—are invariably emphasized, however, and some biographical critiques acknowledge that he is the most significant Anglo-Irish playwright since the prime of Sean O'Casey. A few other reference sources categorize Carroll as the finest Irish dramatist between the O'Casey years and the advent of Brendan Behan. Unquestionably, Carroll suffered because he lacked the charisma of O'Casey or Behan, yet in any sensible estimate of modern Irish drama, Carroll must be rated the most important dramatic talent in the Irish theatre since the early writings of O'Casey.

Carroll has been victimized further by the applause given to these two plays. Although he has written other better-than-average dramas and attempted some plays of considerable philosophical and thematic importance, his other writings have received little scholarly attention, and even the texts of some of his plays (both published and unpublished) have become difficult to locate. Yet his writings deserve and repay serious study and confirm that his position as a highly important figure in contemporary Irish drama cannot fairly be challenged.

Paul Vincent Carroll was born on July 10, 1900, at Blackrock near Dundalk in County Louth, one of the most legend-haunted areas of Ireland. This territory is close to Baile's strand—the locale for many of the ancient Irish heroic episodes—and Carroll's imagination fed on the myths, traditions, and tales that County Louth and its associations quickly brought to mind. In several of his plays he uses these mythic materials both for their symbolic and atmospheric ramifications.

Carroll's father, a country teacher, was a diligent and thorough taskmaster; thus, Carroll—especially well-grounded in the classics, literature, history, and mathematics—received a more than adequate primary education, first at his father's school and then at St. Mary's College, Dundalk. At sixteen Carroll was sent to Dublin to St. Patrick's Training College for teachers, and there Carroll diligently pursued his studies and developed a keen interest in the theatre. In a variety of interviews Carroll has described his youthful fascination with drama: "I used to frequent the Abbey Theatre in my teens and that's how I got to know the ins and outs of the theatre business. The Abbey Theatre, you might say, got to be my spiritual home." Carroll saw in the Abbey "the spiritual rebirth of the Irish race" and regarded the 1916 Easter Rebellion as "the stern realization of these Abbey stage dreams."

Carroll remained in Dublin until 1920 "through tense and dramatic days, saw the lines of tanks crawling down O'Connell Street, saw sharp shooting and quick sudden deaths on the streets, experienced being held up on tramcars and all of us called 'a shower of bloody Irish rebels,' and searched at gunpoint, lived under 'curfew' and martial law," and experienced the frightful and erratic terror caused by the Black and Tans.

In 1920, after the cultural and historical excitement of Dublin life, Carroll returned to his home town. He contemplated becoming an Irish schoolmaster but became considerably disillusioned with provincial existence. In his own words, he "found the family grocers, the publicans and the clergy richer than ever as a result of the war. There was no learning or culture of any kind in the town. No one had ever heard of the Abbey Theatre or of the Irish dramatic or literary revival. They fed the school kiddies on the bathos of the mid-Victorian mamas, and hid from them the works of the poets and writers who were putting Ireland on the international map."

This stagnancy plus the strict clerical control which prevailed in Irish education, as well as low teachers' salaries, persuaded Carroll to emigrate to Glasgow in 1921. There he taught English and mathematics in state schools located in the more economically deprived areas. While he enjoyed teaching, and reports of his dedication were frequent, his interest in writing occupied his spare moments. In Glasgow he wrote and revised plays and sent them to the Abbey Theatre directors for examination and analysis. He became a prolific author of short stories, most of which were published in Scottish periodicals, and also served as a frequent book reviewer for the *Glasgow Herald*.

Carroll's two-act play, *The Watched Pot*, attracted the attention of Yeats and Lennox Robinson and was presented at the experimental Peacock Theatre in Dublin, November 17–24, 1930. This grim drama, set in County Louth, centers about Mick Costello, a dying 83-year-old peasant, and the concern of his daughter-in-law and son to collect the insurance on his life. Carroll later flippantly denigrated the play and attributed its gloominess to Tolstoy, under whose influence he claimed to be. Actually, the influence of Synge is primary. Its brooding, oppressive atmosphere of death is derived directly from *Riders to the Sea*, as is its situation in which an ill man thinks about five of his children who have already died and envisions the death of his sole remaining son.

Dramatic interest in this play drags unduly at times; much of the dialogue is static and repetitious, and although the work relies heavily on dialectal idiom and quaint phraseology, it fails to equal the poetry and lyricism found in Synge's writing. Nevertheless, for a first effort *The Watched Pot* displays considerable promise. Carroll captures starkly the conflict occurring in the family—they desperately need and desire the insurance money, but they feel guilty about hoping for Mick Costello's death. The granddaughter's dilemma is especially well rendered as she gradually changes from horror at the thought of wishing for death and becomes susceptible to her human material desires.

The ability to render convincingly the family's quandary proves that Carroll possessed a raw talent for vigorous realism and perceptive characterization.

At this point Carroll acknowledged two further influences: "fortunately for my work, Ibsen took a sure and disciplined hand in my development, and with the addition of Synge, whose work taught me colour and rhythm, I began to visualize more sanely the strengths and weaknesses of human character."

As Carroll's dramatic activity continued to grow, it became obvious that his more pronounced debt was to Ibsen and the genre of the "well-made play." Like Ibsen, Carroll found problem drama fascinating: he wanted to tackle social, intellectual, religious, and political problems, and he determined to teach and not merely to entertain. In his earliest work he patterned his craftsmanship on the Ibsen-style play; he retained the tight action that held the audience to the drama's climax and attempted to make certain that each scene and character counted.

By the time *Things That Are Caesar's* was produced at the Abbey on August 15, 1932, Carroll's improvement in handling the most popular features of the "well-made play" was strikingly apparent. This drama aroused immediate attention; in fact, the play was chosen by the Abbey Theatre's Irish Players group as the first to be presented on their 1932–1933 American tour. The Abbey Theatre Repertory Company presented *Things That Are Caesar's* at New York City's Martin Beck Theatre on October 18, 1932, less than five weeks after it premiered in Dublin. When the play opened in London in January 1933, Carroll's dramatic reputation had, in less than a year, been successfully launched in the three major centers for English-language drama.

This play's title epitomizes the basic thematic motifs found in most of Carroll's early writing: the conflict between God and Mammon, Church and State, and Flesh and Spirit. Carroll became intrigued by observing these particular forces at work in each individual and determined to ponder the divisions, torments, and tragedies that resulted from such opposing elements in the nature of man.

Julia and Peter Hardy, the protagonists of *Things That Are Caesar's,* exemplify respectively the eternal warfare between the calls of materialism and the demands of mankind's higher spiritual aspirations. While their combined pub and grocery is a financially sound operation, the building's interior especially requires modernization. Julia, legally in charge of the business, determines that she will refurbish and insists that the improvements will not only increase patronage but also bring her to a much higher social level. Status having recently become an obsession of hers, she decides that the money needed for her plans can best be obtained by arranging a marriage between her daughter, Eilish, and the son of Phil Noonan, a successful but vulgar and boorish farmer.

Peter Hardy objects to his wife's schemes because he does not feel that Eilish is ready for marriage (she is presently—at her mother's insistence—attending a convent school) and that the choice of the particular mate in question is most unsuitable. But, above all, Peter does not want his daughter bartered, although he realizes the practice is not uncommon.

Peter is a scholarly, aesthetically sensitive, humane, and good-hearted ex-schoolteacher whose wife's aggressiveness and uncharitableness have caused him to reach the limits of his endurance. When Julia's plans for Eilish are revealed to him, the accumulated insults and slights of many years twist Peter's distaste for his wife into outright hatred; she, in turn, makes no pretense about her antagonism toward him. The daughter becomes the principal object of contention in the now open warfare between husband and wife, both of whom realize that theirs will be a death struggle, since love or reconciliation is impossible where hate has grown and festered for so many years.

In one of the most thorough and biting indictments of a certain type of Irish mother ever presented on the stage, Carroll incisively dissects the thoughts and conniving of the single-minded Julia Hardy, who "can coax, cringe, bully and cry all in the one minute." She can viciously threaten Eilish with physical violence one moment and immediately thereafter become conciliatory and seemingly loving. There is nothing Julia will not make use of in order to obtain her own way. She is a consummate hypocrite and can lie, distort, wear several masks, and change them quickly and with amazing facility. She can calculatingly intrigue for her own welfare but convince the parish priest that all her activities are for Eilish's benefit.

As her husband maintains, Julia can get her way by

rallying the law, the mob, and the priest to her support: "she'll get the Almighty God Himself behind
her!" Julia enlists Father Duffy's assistance when Eilish
refuses to marry Noonan's son, and Eilish finds Father
Duffy's arguments and persuasion extremely difficult
to resist. The priest gives his support and blessing to
compromise, materialism, and mediocrity when he unc-
tuously quotes to Eilish Christ's "Render unto Caesar
the things that are Caesar's" in order to convince her
that marriage is superior to a wish to discover one's
own way and exalt genuine aspirations of the individual spirit. The parish priest ingeniously helps to
bring Eilish to a compromise with materialism and
the mediocre, and he goes about this aim deliberately
and persistently.

Both Julia and Father Duffy maintain that they
represent God's views. In effect, however—as Peter
shrewdly points out—Julia is able to twist God around
and always makes Him agree with her. She justifies
no matter what hypocrisy or trickery she stoops to
as the workings of Divine Providence. She regards herself as a divinely ordained interpreter of God's desires
and will. And Father Duffy, although with more suavity
and gentleness, operates on the same basis.

Dramatically opposed to these unsavory concepts is
the viewpoint Peter Hardy has endeavored to instill
in Eilish. Peter wants his daughter to fulfill her true
nature, to be a free spirit who will grow and become
exalted. Peter hopes she will obtain "vision" and not
be caught and snared in the "stupid nets" of commonplace compromise and mediocrity. He hopes she will

become a "fiery dart pitched forward into the dark to light it." If she is to marry eventually, it hopefully will be for love and not for dowry.

While her father is alive, we are led to believe, Eilish will have the strength and courage to be the master of her own spirit. Even when Peter dies of a heart attack at the end of the second act, he passes away happily because he feels he has won the struggle to save his daughter from the rancid materialism and unhealthy mediocrity that engulf the people of Ireland. Peter has risked the torments of hell in his endeavor to save his daughter, since he defies the Church's morality as it is represented to him.

But when several months pass and the third act opens with the preparations for the wedding of Eilish and Phil Noonan's son, the audience perceives that the mother and the forces of Mammon have won after all. At various times in Act 3 Carroll conveys the impression that Eilish will break the pattern and harken to her dead father's instruction. She quarrels briefly with Father Duffy and notes that he is merciless, that he has no regard for her personal happiness; she is perceptive enough to realize that if she eventually conceives and rears children, he will take them from her and use them to continue the patterns of existence that dominate the thinking of Irish Church and State.

A little later in the same act, when Julia preens herself before a mirror, the carrying of which has brought on Peter's fatal attack, Eilish is repelled by her mother's vulgarity and insensitivity. She rushes off stage after hurling a glass at the mirror, and again it appears that she might escape the mediocre life that awaits her. But Father Duffy calms Julia and knowingly points out that Eilish has now come down the high hill of her dreams and ideals and is now "in the valley." He maintains, quite correctly, to Julia that Eilish "doesn't like it—yet. But she will like it—later on. I can promise you that." Eilish is undoubtedly destined to become in time conventional, uninspired, and, perhaps even distorted: in several ways a duplicate of her mother.

While the obvious tragedy of the situation is all too apparent, the play focuses our attention on a further battlefield. Father Duffy is presented as a representative of the status quo, the spokesman for a rigid and limited view of God and man. Peter Hardy, on the other hand, is a forerunner of a "new Power." Peter asserts that the future conflict between these two views will be the battle for Ireland's future. Genuine brotherly love (unselfish and ideal), individuality and unblighted freedom, high-minded thoughts, and genuine Christ-like attitudes must contend with narrow, bigoted herd-instincts, with hypocrisy and false notions of God and religion, with mediocrity and earthbound obsessions. There is a slight glimmer of hope that Peter Hardy's dreams will eventually come to pass and that "the just God" he invokes before his death is truly on Peter's side, even though Peter's enemies and— Carroll would add—the enemies of high-minded, honorable life have won the day.

Things That Are Caesar's is an absorbing drama, not just in its portrayal of important thematic motifs,

but also in characterization and dialogue. The portrayal of Julia Hardy strikes with especial force. Her
venality and self-righteousness horrify, and her chame-
leon shifts of tone and calculated manipulation of
human lives impress themselves vividly on the mind.
She possesses a spellbinding impact and is credible in
every way. She is destined to defeat her husband because she exists without honor, and in such a combat
complete unscrupulousness must, unfortunately, triumph. Peter's character, competently drawn, suffers in
comparison since goodness cannot withstand such unprincipled treacherousness, and therefore on one level
seems feeble and insufficient.

Father Duffy's character receives a genuinely perceptive representation. The priest understands Eilish's
aspirations, but he believes that these promptings of
the spirit must be brought under control since conformity to the status quo and the workaday world is
for him more in tune with God's design than the fulfillment of individual being. Compromise and expediency will, in Father Duffy's view, save one's soul.
Julia bears witness that much harm and distortion
results from such attitudes, and yet this price the priest
is willing to pay rather than risk overthrowing pious
formulas and time-honored conventions. So ingenious
is Carroll's handling of this character that Duffy
emerges neither as a hero or a villain, but as a
thoroughly understandable proponent of the allegedly
safe and steady way.

This drama, carefully organized in the tradition of
the "well-made play," is also marked by a feature

which becomes a hallmark of Carroll's most notable work, viz., stinging, firm, and precise dialogue. Several of the exchanges between Julia Hardy and her husband are particularly venomous and stirring, and throughout the play the appropriateness of the conversation, especially by Father Duffy and the Noonan family, is distinguished.

The play's one weakness is that the last act, which takes place after the death of the father, tends to be rather tepid and anticlimactic. And yet, unless Eilish were to defy her mother and the priest, it becomes difficult to judge how the letdown in the third act could have been successfully avoided.

Carroll, however, later decided to tamper with and, hopefully, improve the play's final act. A revised form of the drama was published in 1944, twelve years after the play had been first performed. In the new text the third act takes place more than a year after the marriage of Eilish and Terence Noonan. The couple have a child and the business of the "Royal Arms" is quite prosperous. Evident, too, is the fact that Julia Hardy has achieved her materialistic goals.

Despite such encouraging developments, Eilish rebels, refuses to sleep with her husband, shows no interest in her son, and announces that she is going to America and will never return to Ireland. Eilish maintains that now she has attained womanhood and is no longer the mere girl she was before her marriage. She rejects her home and abandons her husband and child, defies Father Duffy and her mother, and seeks freedom and mature fulfillment while escaping from a loveless, materialistic life.

This conclusion, obviously inspired by Carroll's respect for Ibsen and his familiarity with Nora's behavior in *A Doll's House,* possesses considerable dramatic impact. Most startling and forceful, it is designed to terminate the play on a powerful note and to exalt freedom and individuality. Nevertheless, such an ending appears unreal in a 1930s Irish setting. Considering the circumstances revealed in the drama, one tends to doubt that an Irish wife and mother would behave in Eilish's iconoclastic fashion and the audience is not adequately prepared for Eilish's turnabout. Her shocking change of attitude is manipulated by the playwright rather than seeming to rise naturally out of character development. The sensational and melodramatic termination is merely that; it is not a convincing and perfectly credible outgrowth of the drama's events and characterizations.

Carroll has also changed several other elements throughout the later version, ironically making Julia Hardy less domineering and nasty although rendering her more of an alcoholic. The revisions also make the play more episodic and cause the clashes between Julia and her husband to be somewhat less vitriolic. In handling the revisions in the early acts, Carroll's primary concern was to prepare the audience for Eilish's rebellion and ultimate departure from the household; but although he has given her more backbone, individuality, and independence, he still does not satisfactorily convince an audience that she would be capable of eventually deserting her husband and son.

A comparison of the two versions of *Things That Are Caesar's* persuades that, overall, the first text is—despite the rather tranquil and muffled conclusion—a more effective and credible play. The initial stage version contains the essence of realism and truth. Given the Ireland of the period, and given the wiles of the mother and the persuasion of the priest, Eilish's fate is sealed. Even if her father had not died, the mother and the priest would have prevailed. Eilish is not independent or determined enough to guard and maintain the flame of insight her father had left as his legacy. The narrow conventions of Irish society triumph, and the audience contemplates this victory with a realization of the truth of the result, but with a mental and emotional depression that such a result should occur.

Despite this anticlimax, the play demonstrates so much ability and persists in being so generally engrossing that one is disappointed to learn that since the appearance of Carroll's two biggest hits *Things That Are Caesar's* has been consistently overlooked. As Peter Kavanagh (no friend of Carroll's) asserts, the drama was a "new and distinctive kind of contribution. Carroll was the first writer to give the Abbey a play on an anticlerical theme which was handled with such skill that it could give no offense." Kavanagh also noted that "rarely in the history of the Abbey had any play received such enthusiastic applause." And J. J. Hayes, writing from Dublin for the *New York Times*, declared: "It may . . . be said with truth that the recent staging of *Things That Are Caesar's,* the winning play in the Abbey competition, constitutes the most important event in the history of the national theatre since Sean O'Casey sprang into overnight fame ten years ago." Hayes would not then conjecture about Carroll's subsequent development, but he concluded: "Suffice it to say that, with his initial play, he has scored heavily."

II

The critical success of *Things That Are Caesar's*
convinced Carroll that his desire to pursue a playwriting career was not an *ignis fatuus*. He continued to
teach in Scotland and write until the popularity of
Shadow and Substance gave him the financial opportunity to resign from the Scottish public school system
and devote his full energies to the theatre.

Shadow and Substance arouses immediate attention
because of its crisp, pungent dialogue and its expertly
drawn characters. Canon Skerritt and Brigid, the youthful serving girl who works in the Canon's rectory,
draw the focal interest, but schoolmaster Dermot
O'Flingsley also becomes a fully realized creation and
part of a three-character interrelation. Carroll acknowledged that the Canon's character was inspired by Jonathan Swift: "For years I had been studying the Au-
gustan period of English literature, and have always
been fascinated by its chief character—Dean Swift. I
decided to resurrect Dean Swift, make him not only
a Catholic but a learned interpreter of Catholicism,
and throw him into the modern mental turmoil in
Ireland."

The Canon is scarred by excessive pride. Although his father was Irish, his mother came from a Spanish background. Skerritt frequently visits Spain, where he moves gracefully and opulently among the aristocracy. He prefers the finest wines and holds himself high above his fellow priests and parishioners. He disdains contact with farmers and anyone associated with the working class, ridicules Irish football, tea drinking, and almost everything distinctly Irish.

Educated in the ideals of Latin classicism and being a world traveller, he inveighs against the steady decline of classic ideals. He insists that the false ideals of Nordic civilization are corrupting people throughout the world. He believes that the new Nordic "financial scoundrelism" has "vulgarized our reading, our music, our art, our very privacy." The Canon is particularly outraged when his assistant priests hang up in the rectory a gaudy oleograph of the Sacred Heart. When the curates protest that nearly all the pictures in the house are really secular, the Canon proclaims his concern with grace and beauty. He declares: "If, for a moment, I felt our Redeemer's heart was akin to that monstrosity on the wall, I should go back to Socrates, and be a pagan." He orders the picture removed and suggests that it be placed along a roadway to give the people some idea of how the "Royal Christ of the Renaissance" has been debased.

The Canon continually denounces emotionalism in religious matters and maintains that Catholicism "rests on a classical, almost abstract love of God." When later it is discovered that O'Flingsley has pseudonymously written a book censuring the deficiencies of the Irish Church, the Canon wisely rejects any protests against the author in a calm but sarcastic manner. The Canon maintains that if the book in question had been written by an author of scholarship and classic status, then it might become a source of alarm

> especially when we have presently no known Irish Catholic scholar with that delicacy of touch, subtlety of culture and profundity of classical knowledge to defend and even rescue the Church intellectually. Coming in contact with such an immaturity as this the insufficiently scholared mind, fed mostly on sentimentalisms in the form of learning, is often shocked, and—vulgarly agitated. Violent emotionalism results, followed by a quite ridiculous hubbub, tawdry heroics, even bigoted physical violence under holy names, and generally a quite ludicrous procedure that the classic dignity of the mind of the Church recoils from.

O'Flingsley also believes that he exists on a plateau above the people, and in general treats them with scorn. Embittered, critical, cynical, impatient, but aspiring for educational and cultural improvement and deeply steeped in ideals which are being rooted out because of conditions in Irish society, O'Flingsley finally derives the courage to give up his position as a lackey schoolmaster, "a Canon's yeoman," and to set out and seek a new career, even though he is stigmatized by having written an anti-clerical book, and may find it difficult to obtain another position in Ireland.

Although the Canon and the schoolmaster are antagonists, they both deeply admire and respect Brigid, the young housekeeper. She in turn is filled with admiration and love for them but is aware of their over-weening *hubris.* Gentle, kindly, saintly—a person of complete trust and innocence—Brigid has deep devotion and a very real resemblance to her religious name-sake. The young girl claims to have visions of St. Brigid, who was born in the Dundalk area—Carroll's boyhood home and the locale of the play. Among the mystical revelations received by Brigid is that the Canon must humble himself and obtain a deeper faith and love for people. The Saint's message also indicates that O'Flingsley should give up his blunder-ing pride and put love in his heart, though O'Flingsley professes to be too disillusioned and bitter to believe in love.

Brigid attempts to serve as a mediator between the two male disputants and to instill in them more hu-mane attitudes, but throughout the major part of the play her holiness and simple saintliness cannot influ-ence them sufficiently. Only when Brigid is acci-dentally killed while endeavoring to protect O'Flings-ley from a mob attack do the two men come to hu-mility and a heartfelt awareness of the need for simple faith and genuine love. The Canon, in particular, who had exhibited the most pride and snobbishness, feels the deficiencies in his character and the gross nature of his spiritual shortcomings.

According to Paul Vincent Carroll's own interpre-tation, the most important question raised by the play involves the Canon's attitudes of pride, snobbism, aloof-ness, and distaste for the mediocrity and vulgarity about him. The saintly innocence of Brigid, however, penetrates to the inner turmoil endured by the pastor: "No one really knows him but poor innocent Brigid, for even if he is proud and haughty, she has seen the tears on his cheeks. She knows that his tears and his secret humility are forever fighting a losing battle with his pride." But, Carroll avers, Brigid is aware that in one way or another he will be saved because "she loves him above and beyond the flesh, with a love that will give all and ask for nothing." And this is exactly what happens; her accidental death results in his complete humanization. In her idealistic simplicity, her holy innocence, and her unselfish love Brigid appears to have attained the secret of existence, while much of the Canon's propriety is seen to be practically meaningless because of his corrupting pride. Goodness and simple faith, Carroll maintains, are ultimately superior to rigid asceticism and aloof classicism. The child then is closer to the secret of life than the scholar. Human beings must not expect the world to improve through such extraneous matters as education or a particular form of government. The heart of man, not externals, must change: Brigid speaks of "God's hint to man to build in the heart forever and ever, instead of with stone and mortar and . . . pride."

Brigid symbolizes the essential need of Ireland (indeed of all countries and people everywhere), but she is surrounded on all sides by individuals who mar the ideal. On this level, Brigid represents the genuine national spirit crushed by conflicting forces; and the Canon, the curates, and the mob stirred up against O'Flingsley symbolize uncharitably rigid formal religion while, in Carroll's words, the schoolmaster represents "a rebellious breaking away from parochialism in education."

The play assumes added effectiveness because the portraits of the minor characters strike as forcefully in their way as the analysis of the Canon and the main forces of conflict. Fathers Corr and Kirwan are expertly captured in all their vulgar awkwardness and banality. They confuse religion and holiness with sports, motor cars, and even with going about prescribing cures for old ladies' rheumatics. Emotionalism and sentimentalism dominate their lives so that neither their minds nor hearts can be lifted to more aspiring and worthy possibilities.

The two new teachers who will assume control of the parish school are observed to be almost childish. Thomasina is a shallow, scatterbrained "dumpling who reeks eternally of peppermints" while Francis O'Connor is a cringing spineless booby fit only to be "a piece of furniture in a chapel house." No documentary condemnation of the weaknesses of the Irish school system could be as telling as the system viewed in the guise of these two practitioners. The teachers are manipulated and dominated completely by clerical administrators and must be willing to bow and scrape before every clerical whim or demand. They are forced to become lackeys; otherwise, their position is terminated. Ireland appears to have no place in teaching for O'Flingsley. The humanitarian rebel is stripped of his job and really run out of town. Instead of accepting legitimate criticism and attempting to improve conditions, the men in control of education stifle and suppress all dissent.

All of these materials are presented in the Ibsen formula of a tightly constructed play with intensely probing character revelation. But Carroll's ability with dialogue is his own gift. The conversation is quick-paced, concise, sharp, and frequently ironic, satiric, and humorous. Several of the dialogue exchanges are as keen and as lively as any conversations conceived by a modern dramatist. The Canon's trenchant satiric barbs while speaking with his two curates, Thomasina, Francis O'Connor, and Miss Cooney intrigue an audience, and several "great scenes" appear throughout; the bitter exchange between the Canon and O'Flingsley in the third act is perhaps the most memorable. The drama critics, who enthusiastically applauded the play, used such comments as "passionate eloquence," "probing power," "spiritual beauty," and "tender and sensitive," but the play is also masterly for its adept use of satire and irony. It possesses an astringency that both bites and purifies.

Like O'Casey in his anti-clericism and like Synge in his attack on Irish characteristics, Carroll tried to capture all that he found distasteful in Ireland and to present these aspects on the stage. In something of a rhetorical overstatement, Micheal MacLiammoir (writing in Lennox Robinson's anthology *The Irish Theatre*) tries to enumerate all of them:*

Shadow and Substance, indeed, hits very hard at our worst faults, and what is alarming is that all of these

---

* Reprinted with permission of Macmillan London and Basingstoke.

are not only recognisable to an honest Irishman, they are characteristic, and are to be met everywhere with a startling frequency. The glaring defects of ignorance, sluttishness, bigotry, contrariness, are all here, together with that peculiarly typical and exasperating trick of deliberate, self-conscious, arch, unblushing, brazen, whimsy, sickening, prudish, presumptuous affectation of innocence, purity, childlike playfulness of heart, that astounding glorification of incompetence, and that ghastly "Sure I'm hopeless, but amn't I irresistible?" attitude with which every dweller in Ireland is familiar, . . .

While the play has aspects that are rather peculiarly Irish, it is not simply an Irish play. In speaking to John McClain, Carroll remarked, "Like Ibsen, I use common places and common characters, and I try, by the strength of the writing, to lift them from the commonplace to the universal." *Shadow and Substance* achieves this intended goal. It establishes that pride, violence, intolerance, and similar abominations are false and vicious shadows compared with the essential substance of fundamental faith and humanity.

Carroll's next play, *The White Steed,* was rejected by the Abbey because the directors of Ireland's foremost theatre believed the play to be too anticlerical. After the play opened on Broadway and ultimately received the unanimous approval of the New York Drama Critics as the best foreign play of the 1938–39 season, Carroll wrote a vitriolic letter to the *Irish Times* in which he expressed his especial bitterness at the Abbey's rejection since he was anxious to enhance the Abbey's reputation as well as his own.

Carroll bases the concept of *The White Steed* on an ancient Irish legend dealing with Ossian, the son of

Finn. (William Butler Yeats gave a poetic version of
the legend in his "The Wanderings of Oisin" [1889],
and it is obvious that Carroll has studied Yeats's work.
In fact, the motto of the play—"You are still wrecked
among heathen dreams"—is uttered by St. Patrick in
Yeats's poem in the course of the dialogue between
Patrick and Oisin.) According to the saga, Ossian,
out hunting on a particular day, meets a most beautiful girl astride an impressive white horse. This girl's
name is Niam and she manages to persuade Ossian to
accompany her to the land of Eternal Youth. There
Ossian receives all his wishes, including the love of
Niam. But after 300 years he begins to think of life
on earth and desires to return to see how the earth
has progressed during his absence. Niam warns him,
however, that if he returns, he must not touch the
earth.

When he arrives in Ireland and searches for Finn
and the gallant heroes of past times, he discovers that
they have vanished. Now the land is inhabited by
countless numbers of small black-haired men. St. Patrick warns Ossian that unless he repents he will be
sent to hell to join his pagan ancestors. Ossian defies
Patrick's admonition and determines that he would
rather be in the company of his gallant forebears in
hell than be joined with the country's present inhabitants in a heaven of small-minded and unheroic men.
(Again one recognizes Carroll's closeness to Yeats!)
One day he reaches down from the saddle of his white
steed to help several of the little men lift an extremely
heavy block of marble. As he raises the marble, his
saddle breaks and Ossian falls to earth. As soon as he

touches the soil hundreds of years come upon him, and he withers wretchedly and disappears from view.

Carroll takes this legend and works it into modern dramatic action set in his favorite locale, County Louth. Canon Matt Lavelle, the aged pastor of a village church, suffers a sudden paralysis presumably brought on by a stroke. A young priest named Shaughnessy is assigned by the bishop to take full charge of the parish while the Canon is recuperating. The play immediately and sharply focuses on Shaughnessy's character. He is a rabid Puritan who is opposed to drinking, dancing, and romancing. He organizes a committee of vigilant citizens who are instructed to spy on their neighbors and report any behavior they deem in any way improper. Shaughnessy, in his bigoted and misplaced zeal, turns the situation into a kind of mass witch-hunt with the concomitant hysteria, foolishness, and injustice of such activities. Father Shaughnessy is completely merciless and rigidly dogmatic. He regards all state and local governments as subordinate to the Church and expects the police to yield even in matters secular. He threatens the schoolmaster Denis Dillon by insisting that unless Dillon stops dating a Protestant girl, he will be dismissed from his position, and Denis yields to this clerical pressure. Father Shaughnessy also has youthful Nora Fintry dismissed from her position as librarian.

It is to Carroll's credit that he controls the dramatic structure of the play tightly so that we watch Father Shaughnessy with gradually increasing fascination. His demands and obsession for power increase in crescendo so that each new scene in which he appears paints him in darker colors, while the contrasts with the Canon's views are continually underscored. Both men are convincingly characterized, and their conflict must bring them to an ultimate confrontation.

Nora Fintry rebels against Father Shaughnessy and his vigilante supporters, and after much persuasion she convinces Denis Dillon to join her. They are both in danger of being dragged off by a mob of Shaughnessy's supporters when Canon Lavelle intervenes. He has miraculously regained his ability to walk, albeit with the aid of a cane. He manages to restore order and tranquillity. The Canon offers Dillon his job back, but Nora refuses to allow this since Denis would once more, even if benignly under the Canon, be subservient to clerical domination. She wants to free Denis, to exalt his individuality. She is Niam, born out of the race of ancient Irish warriors, poets, saints, and heroes. She is the past spirit of Ireland who will not accept servitude. The Canon encourages Dillon with the words: "go, Denis, and even if she wants you up on a pagan steed, get right beside her. It will not take you astray—her white steed has not come down the centuries for nothing." In fact, as Nora tells Denis in Act 2, "Every man . . . must lift himself on the white steed."

There emerges in much of Carroll's work a longing for the ancient pagan past. At that period, Carroll fantasizes, Ireland and its people were much more grand and heroic and filled with vigor and joy—qualities that have declined in the ensuing centuries. In Carroll's view the legendary past becomes a golden age which haunts most sensitive and thoughtful contemporary Irishmen and forces them to make invidious comparisons with the present and to yearn for a re-creation of these ancient virtues. A line from Yeats used as the motto for *The White Steed*—"You are still wrecked among heathen dreams"—becomes a re-curring note linking past and present Ireland and the conscious and unconscious hopes and aspirations of its present inhabitants.

Before the play received its premiere in New York, Carroll wrote a long explanation of the symbolism. In part, he declared:

> I have created an old man who lives by faith alone [Canon Lavelle]; a sterner type of man who believes in rules and strict discipline [Father Shaughnessy], a younger man who has come fearfully out of the centuries, dumb and hungry [Dillon], and a girl [Nora Fintry] who lives by instinct kept pure by a dreaming and a vivid sense of the indestructible beauty of the world. The white steed is to her who has read of it the symbol of truth and beauty, and the little black men in the ancient story are rediscovered by her in the modern world in the guise of those hordes of driven humanity who are denied the right to think for themselves, denied the right to laugh and be glad they are alive, the right to dream of hidden loveliness and the ageless foolishness of humanity.

Canon Lavelle emerges as an immensely likable and desirable cleric—probably the most believable yet ap-pealing priest ever created by an Irish dramatist. He possesses a shrewd knowledge of human nature and intimately understands his parishioners and their ways. He further realizes that one person has to be treated somewhat differently from another. He behaves in this eclectic manner, innocently bribing one individual and cozening another, taking a little graft in the form of free butter, and baptizing the child of a woman who is not in good standing with the Church. He holds a deep and abiding faith in God, but also extols tolerance, forgiveness, kindliness, and generosity. His religious views are firmly rooted, but they are benevolent and loving.

Vis-a-vis the Canon, Father Shaughnessy appears to be almost an unreal monster, except for the fact that history proves the existence of such fanatics. In his complete disregard for common humanity and a tolerant reasonableness, Father Shaughnessy demonstrates the dangers of dogmatic and singleminded ruthlessness. He is without so much as an iota of humor whereas the Canon is bubbling with wit and joy. Father Shaughnessy's portrayal again supports the universality of Carroll's intentions, since the struggle for tolerance, common sense, and reasonable freedom is one that would be familiar in any other country at almost all times.

In an interview given to the *New York Sun,* Carroll declared that in *The White Steed* he tried "to prove that we must, at all costs, get back to the humanity in our life; we must stop devising laws which hurt people. It is a plea for personal freedom." In another newspaper commentary Carroll asserts that he desires this drama to interpret "a phase not only of the changing in Ireland but of the changing world about it. I remember that besides being brave I must be humorous, and besides being just I must have humanity and equanimity."

Again, Carroll has created vivid characters and sharply honed, astringent dialogue. Some of the pitfalls of the "well-made play" can, however, be observed here. The audience tends to suspect that the Canon will eventually come to save the day. The rather miraculous recovery from his paralysis is attributed to the Canon's prayers and religious faith, but there is more than a bit of the "deus ex machina" involved in the Canon's timely recovery. The same fault can be noticed when Denis Dillon eventually attains courage and mettle after he has been a weak-willed drinker throughout much of the play. It appears that Carroll is forcing a romantic ending between Dillon and Nora that is not logically acceptable.

It is further evident that the play could actually have pronounced its basic themes without the symbolism of Ossian and Niam. *Things That Are Caesar's* and *Shadow and Substance* both had a persuasive clarity, and the few symbols that were used achieved unity with the play. *The White Steed* might not have had so poetic an aura if the Ossian-Niam episode were not incorporated, but the basic power of the play would have remained unchanged. A tendency to obfuscate the material with allegory and symbolism will become a growing characteristic of much of Paul Vincent Carroll's future work. It especially harms his next two plays, *Kindred* and *The Old Foolishness,* both conceived on a grand scale, but both made unwieldly and murky by involved and excessive concern with symbolism.

III

In 1939 *Kindred,* Carroll's most ambitious and most philosophical drama, was produced in Dublin and New York. In this play Carroll sought to illustrate the thesis that "there is something stronger than blood joining people together no matter what their face, race or outlook" and that "the real leaders of the world should be artists, not the politicians or religious divines."

Quite apparent from many interviews and comments given by Carroll to newspapers in Ireland and in the United States was the fact that the author felt intensely about his theme and that he earnestly believed that the artist remained the only hope for the world's salvation. Carroll recommended that "the creative mind" should "rule the world." He declared that this development was vital "because the politicians and the financiers have plunged the world into war again, and the church is helpless to prevent it. It is time for creative minds to ascend to rulership. The creative minds have no axe to grind, no country, no flag, no class."

Carroll attempted to illustrate this hypothesis by

writing a five-scene play during which a time gap of 25 years was to pass between the events in the first two episodes and the happenings in the last three sections. The first two scenes focus on an irascible artist named Dermot O'Regan and his beloved, Mary Griffin. Dermot has no wish to marry or have children. He insists that a son of his could never become one of the common crowd; he "could never fit himself to count coins, or be an ironmonger or a grocer, and the crowd would tramp over him. Then he would curse us both." Dermot gives Mary a very beautiful picture he has painted of her and forces her to leave, recommending that she marry someone else. He asserts that he has instructed Mary in a special sense of beauty and given her the inspiration all individuals require.

Dermot talks about a mysterious "destiny" planned for him, and while he waits for this mission to be fulfilled, hoping that he will be instrumental in rescuing "the Almighty Artist" and winning "back Heaven from the Junkers," strange, ghostly, other-worldly Figures appear to him and declare that he must propagate so that an offspring carrying on their and Dermot's philosophy will be available. Dermot produces the required child by having sexual relations with a vulgar and unappealing servant. (Traces of Yeats's dramas are observable here, particularly reflected in the "lecher-saint theme" found in such a play as *A Full Moon in March,* where promiscuity is regarded as a necessary condition for the arrival of a future hero.) Upon learning that a child has been conceived, Dermot promptly commits suicide.

The break to 25 years in the future is abrupt and distracting. Mary Griffin has married a local grocer and pub-keeper, Robert Fenet, but she seems to have more interest in a handyman named Dermot O'Regan (the illegitimate son of Mary's first love) than in her own schoolmaster son Michael. Michael thinks of being elected to Parliament, but he is not at all interested in helping the poor people of his election district. He wishes only to frolic in Dublin and to gather as much money and personal prestige from politics as possible. Mary laments to Dermot that Michael has disappointed and distressed her. She had dreamed of her son "being a poet or a writer among his own people; one who would stay with them and lift them up and make them conscious of their finer selves."

The Strange Figures again appear and try to instill their magic and creative inspiration in Michael as he sleeps. The Figures deeply disturb the complacent Michael, and a subsequent conversation with Dermot causes him to perceive and understand things he had not previously noticed. Dermot and Mary hope that Michael will decide to continue schoolteaching and by so doing "raise up one greater than himself," since "in each of us there is that power, and in the using of it lies the salvation of Earth and Heaven."

Michael, then, must choose between philistinism and political chicanery on the one hand and devotion to artistic ideals on the other. For a time, hope appears that Michael might be willing to make the more idealistic decision, but the influence of his father and his fiancée prevails, and Michael turns to mediocrity and political expediency.

Mary's disappointment is considerably assuaged by
her "spiritual" son, Dermot, who stresses that they are
kindred, the type of kindred "that outlasts the kindred
of the blood." Dermot predicts that someone like
Mary will, in the future, give birth to a son who will
far surpass others and perform the wonderful feats
that Michael failed to assay.

This concept ties Carroll to Yeats, Joyce, AE, and
numerous other modern Irish writers who were obsessed with the desire for heroism is an unheroic world.
Kindred demonstrates that Carroll was well-acquainted
with a concept stressed in several of Yeats's plays; viz.,
that the gods must have human assistance before they
can achieve their purposes. Furthermore, *Kindred*'s
search for a new leader reflects the general Messianic
ideal among Irish writers who were preoccupied with
the heroic personality and with heroic ideals for Ireland. Herbert Howarth has eloquently discussed this
search in his *Irish Writers 1880–1940,* noting that the
Irish literary movement was shaped not only by the ex-
pression of rebellion but also by the hope for a great
leader, a man of destiny who would both succor the
oppressed and bring redemption. In his portrayal of
heroism and heroic qualities—in various forms—Carroll
returns again and again to this theme in several of his
plays, *Kindred* being his most philosophically gran-
diose statement of such conceptions.

Unfortunately, both for Carroll's high thinking and
for his career, *Kindred* fails as a play—for several reasons. It is too often melodramatic, artificial, and stagey
—at times almost wooden. These aspects particularly
dominate the opening two scenes when Mary and Der-

mot Sr. are on stage. Mary is presented as too dominated, worshipful, and servile while the older Dermot, who is supposed to be representative of artistic genius, is excessively frenzied and bizarre in speaking and behaving. He is choleric and overbearing. He claims to be a madman and behaves like one. Dermot's mysticism and special powers do not ring true. As portrayed, he does not appear to have the ability to make Mary see mystical things.

In addition to the unreal characterizations, the dialogue is generally stiff and unreal, sometimes flat and platitudinous, occasionally even banal; for example: "Let me just look at you . . . Do with me what you like . . . Make me even your amusement." This play contains the most inept dialogue Carroll ever wrote. Mary and Dermot Sr. seem to be purely synthetic creatures having no relation to actual flesh and blood people. In the first two segments of the play they speak as if they were strange artificial creatures from some amateurish nineteenth-century melodrama.

The second part of *Kindred,* comprising the last three scenes, improves, but still the play remains unreal. Scene Three's ending when Dermot Jr. discovers that Mary had loved his father and then declares that they are kindred seems hollow, highly contrived, and mannered in effect.

Another deficiency is illustrated in the portrayal of young Dermot. Dermot's son appears to be no more stable than his father. He frequently growls and rages, and on one occasion even threatens to kill Michael's fiancée by hurling her off a bridge. He exemplifies

mostly cynicism, grouchiness, and irascibility, and utters several pronouncements denouncing "trust and
love and honour." If Dermot represents one of the
artistic types allegedly on the path that will lead to
saving the world, then it would appear that the world
is indeed more lost than ever.

Carroll's thesis as presented in this drama stands
unproven, exaggerated, and simply incredible. The abstractions and the mysticism are too remote and too
fantastic to be taken seriously. Despite a few adequate
passages in the play's last two scenes, *Kindred* is defi-
nitely cloudy and quite disorganized in both approach
and theme. In fact the play's soaring hypothesis that
the world needs a unity of creative minds to replace
nationalism and the wars resulting from it is really
completely submerged and lost. *Kindred* furnishes little
support for the concept that the creative minds should
now rule and that such minds, as Carroll remarked
in a pre-premiere interview, "will give us a decent life."

When *Kindred* closed on Broadway after a run of
only two weeks, Carroll gave a newspaper interview
in which he agreed with the critics who had faulted
the drama. Carroll explained that he "lost control" of
his characters and that they "did and said things [he]
had no intention of letting them do or say." Carroll
noted:

> You are absolutely right in saying that I started out to
> prove one thing and instead ended up by proving an-
> other. This was my theory. It is the artist, the creative
> artist, who should be the ruling force in humanity, not
> the blind and petty and domineering politician. By
> artist I didn't mean the vagabond fiddler I drew in the

character of Dermot O'Regan. I mean the man who conceives and builds bridges, or beautiful ships, or who
contributes in any way to the beauty of life.

Carroll later remarked that he had unconsciously
drawn O'Regan as "intolerant and hateful," and that
O'Regan's bitterness rendered him unsympathetic. This
handling of O'Regan "put me in a position of having
my protagonist appear rather as a symbol of evil than
of good." Carroll's comments distinguish themselves
for perception and accuracy, and his dissatisfaction with
the play was to become a commonplace in dramatic
circles.

Ironically, too, the character of Robert Fenet, Mary's
husband, who was to be the principal villain, is portrayed with a rounded touch of humanity. After the
play failed, Carroll also realized that he had mis-
handled this important character. In Fenet

> I intended to put all the petty, mean qualities of a
> shriveled soul, making him the epitome of the evil against
> which Dermot O'Regan would do battle. And again,
> when his real character developed, I discovered that he
> was actually a nice lovable little chap despite his faults,
> and the audience was put in the rather comical dilemma
> of having to like the villain and despise the hero.

It is startling that Carroll did not realize Robert
Fenet's humanity sooner since he gives him such lines
as: "We've got to live life, and life is a rusty mare
that's always luckleppin', not a fairy boat on a lake.
Your mother can tell you that. She had dreams, too,
but they didn't keep her from weighin' butter and
countin' eggs, and scrubbin' shelves. And the dreams

she crucified in her to make a little home with an
oul' fluther like me, were finer than any you'll ever
have." Fenet also shows physical affection for Mary,
calls her by such gentle terms as "soft-heart," and is
genuinely devoted to his son.

Even the pragmatic politician, J. K. Keefe, for all
his political maneuvering and expediency, does not
strike the audience or reader with the negative conno-
tations associated with the two Dermots.

Carroll arrived at the conclusion that he had learned
valuable lessons as a result of *Kindred*'s failure, the
most penetrating awareness being that he must force
himself in his playwriting to seek "clarity and lucidity."
He added, "I do believe in symbolism, for the only
method I know of portraying certain human forces
on the stage is through symbols. But the symbols must
be clear and unmistakable."

That the play's theme and failure continued to obsess
Carroll is evidenced by the fact that in the 1950s he
spent much time writing a considerably revised version
of the play, which he titled *The Secret Kindred*. This
new changed form demonstrates vast improvement and
establishes that the subject matter and thesis were
capable of yielding a better play than the one Carroll
initially wrote.

The first noticeable development in the revised
script is a firm, definite tightening of the play's structure. This effect is achieved primarily by eliminating
the 25-year break between the second and third sections. Now Carroll works entirely from a present-day
setting and reveals the early relationship between Mary

and the senior Dermot in several short flashbacks which are smooth, component parts of the play.

The portrait of Dermot Sr. is softened, and he is presented as not only an intuitive artistic genius but also as a truly poetic spirit. Even though he still retains some of his gruffness and thoughtlessness, he achieves credibility: in spite of his artistic eccentricities he arouses a measure of sympathy from the audience. His portrayal and the naturalness with which the flashbacks are handled strengthen the historical associations of the drama.

Carroll has also immeasurably changed the portraits of the representatives of business and politics so that they become scoundrelly, but in a most human, non-exaggerated fashion. In the revised form of the play, Robert Fenet is shown to be greedy, dictatorial, and corrupt. The knavery and unprincipled maneuvering of Fenet and political boss J. K. Keefe are sharply and bitingly revealed. Bribery, hyprocrisy, and expedient double-dealing are not only practiced by Fenet and Keefe but condoned and encouraged by them as normal and proper behavior. The sharp indictment of these forces, to which Mary and the younger Dermot are opposed, gives this version of the play more focus and markedly draws the lines of division.

Also greatly improved is the presentation of the conflict Mary's son, Michael, faces. Michael must acutely meditate upon and wrestle with a choice of careers, and he broods and ponders his problem at length. In the original play Michael gave the issue relatively little thought. He was too quickly enticed by the opportunity of obtaining prestige, power, and money which a political career would open to him. His ultimate decision was easily predicted. In *The Secret Kindred,* however, the audience is kept in definite doubt about Michael's final decision until near the very end. The pressures of the mysterious Figures, the influence of Dermot, and a more thoughtful realization of his mother's spiritual strength and goals give him much pause and torment him with anguished reflections. Michael understands his mother's hope and longing that he will dedicate himself to Ireland and its people and help raise them to higher goals, showing them "their splendid souls." As Mary points out, the people need a new *social* leader, not another political leader. They require "someone a little like Christ who would . . . lift them up to the finer values . . . the glory that was once Ireland! And look at them now! Lost music . . . lost art . . . lost nobility. . . . We just export them now to be the labourers, bartenders and domestic servants of Britain and America."

Michael comes to understand fully the perfidy and corruption of his father and the politicians. His father feels that Michael is behaving like an innocent child and foolish idealist who doesn't know the facts of life. When Michael attempts to impress upon his father the importance of truth, Fenet makes a mockery of what he regards as nonexistent. He argues that people live by favoritism, nepotism, by graft and compromise, by false words and hollow promises. Politicians like J. K. Keefe control matters and operate in much the same manner as the businessmen. They mislead and trick the people and exist by duplicity. Slander and Red-baiting become the ultimate weapon, and any under-handed trick or practice is allowable provided it succeeds.

Michael further comes to recognize that his fiancée, Agnes—J. K.'s daughter—is shallow, insensitive, and self-seeking and that she lacks such vital and humane qualities as "nobility in the heart" and "love of humility." The contrast between Mary, the mother, and Agnes, the fiancée, is defined and delineated incisively. The sensitive, deeply spiritual, and suffering Mary (in many ways a modern form of Christ's mother) perceives meanings beyond the façade of ordinary existence. On the other hand, the superficial and utterly pragmatic Agnes sees only the surface of things. The former represents the spiritual, the latter the material. Both aspects magnetize Michael and pull him in opposite directions.

But at least Michael comes to recognize his choice clearly. He observes that both political parties are corrupt and decadent and realizes that the most honorable and idealistic decision would be to inaugurate a new independent political party that would commence with pure motives and build upon a fresh, honest foundation. Such a movement would present Michael with the opportunity and moral force to do something unselfish and helpful for the impoverished and for the country as a whole. But, ultimately and sadly, Michael proves too weak and earthbound for heroism and worthwhile dedication.

While the extreme disappointment of both Mary and

Dermot becomes evident (they had thought Michael capable of higher goals and of heroic strength), their belief that Truth will gradually dawn upon the world gives a forceful and meaningful conclusion to the play, the undefeated hope of the two kindred spirits contrasting sharply with a crescendo of political enthusiasm as Michael's candidacy is reaffirmed to the crowds. Thus *The Secret Kindred* ends with considerably more irony and emotion than was true of the first version. The two opposing views of life juxtapose vividly as the music of a brass band supporting Michael's political campaign moves out of hearing range while Dermot appears dishevelled and begrimed, a fugitive from the police, but still exalting the ideal. Michael has become a modern Judas, while Dermot is an imperfect harbinger of those who will yet arrive and offer salvation to the people.

In *The Secret Kindred* Carroll considerably improved the original dramatic materials and themes. If this version had appeared in 1939 he would have achieved a qualified success. *The Secret Kindred* proves that Carroll wrote *Kindred* much too hurriedly and carelessly and neglected to think out the best means of presenting a complex, ambitious theme. The revised version contains generally effective dialogue (the conversational blunders found in *Kindred* are neatly avoided), plus penetrating characterization, and a cohesively presented conflict of views rage throughout the play. Nevertheless, three weaknesses seem almost immediately apparent.

First, too many sections of the play are excessively

didactic and preachy. In his eagerness to convey his thesis, Carroll overstates most of his points. Consequently, what on some occasions should be subtle is heavily stressed and what is apparent is too often repeated and underscored.

Secondly, the appearance and actions of the mysterious other-worldly Figures cause disorientation—as they did in the original version. While they are now presented with more credibility than in *Kindred,* they remain ambivalent in relation to the play. On the one hand they are attention-arresting devices, adding suspense and further tension. They also help the play focus firmly on the issues at stake and upon Michael's dilemma. On the other hand, they appear too unreal and ethereal for the time and material of the play. As symbols they are not really compatible with the materials and demands of an essentially realistic play. They represent ghosts out of the past and are designated by such terms as "men of the seashore" and "Beachcombers on the eternal shores." While the reason for their creation and appearance become obvious since some such spiritual force and continuity aiming toward a kindred of the creative must be shown as operative, the Figures do not become vivid enough in their own right.

A third reservation persists, and this concerns a characteristic of the original script. Carroll's thesis depends on such exalted, inspiring—but questionable— notions as Shelley's belief that the "poets and writers are the unacknowledged legislators of the race." While Carroll would broaden the terms to include musicians, architects, etc., one still has doubts about creative, artistic minds bringing about world peace and justice. As Brooks Atkinson, one of the doubters, once pointed out, many artists and creative minds have supported totalitarian governments and advocated individual repression. Creative ability and artistry are no guarantee of goodness and purity of intention or behavior. Indeed, Dermot O'Regan himself, while admittedly just a forerunner of those who are to come, is—despite his ability to play the violin expertly and to compose lilting, original folksongs—perhaps the best refutation of Carroll's thesis. For the purposes of this play at least Carroll appears to be preaching a form of evolutionary utopianism which he expects one day to dawn on earth. In the light of world history and the evil tendencies rooted within each person, Carroll's millenarian proposals require more persuasive power to be convincing than the *Kindred* plays furnish.

Before considering Carroll's next play, a word needs to be said about Peter Kavanagh's account of Carroll in his widely circulated *The Story of the Abbey Theatre*. Kavanagh ends his brief essay on Carroll with some comments on *Kindred,* for in Kavanagh's view the failure of *Kindred* is deemed the central point of Carroll's career. Kavanagh's opinions have caused much of the neglect that Carroll's work has faced in the last 25 years, yet his notions are so obviously prejudiced and wrong-headed that they should have been immediately suspect.

Besides censuring Carroll's alleged excessive egotism and arrogance and denigrating the playwright further

by unnecessarily sneering at his small physical stature
and his "bald head," Kavanagh even faults *Shadow and
Substance,* one of his astounding cavils being that the
play is defective because Carroll did not have the dying
Brigid receive the last sacraments of the Church. The
height of insult is reached, however, when Kavanagh
specifically blames the failure of *Kindred* (and therefore Carroll) for the Abbey's decline. In his interpre-
tation, "A major dramatist was needed at just that
time [1939], and had Carroll developed in that direc-
tion the Abbey might have been saved for another
generation." Yet Kavanagh ignores other aspects of the
situation and makes light of the fact that the Abbey
in the previous year had rejected a major play by
Carroll, *The White Steed.* It appears much more plau-
sible that the short-sighted and somewhat questionable
practices and policies of the Abbey's directors—which
are indicated in Joseph Holloway's journal of the Irish
theatre during this period and discussed especially in
Robert Hogan's *After the Irish Renaissance*—discour-
aged and even stifled several potential dramatic voices.
To a great degree the Abbey directors themselves
brought on the theatre's decline, and they, together
with such difficulties as censorship—which caused Frank
O'Connor to resign from the Abbey board in 1939—
and problems caused by World War II, for instance,
were the real culprits and not the failure of Carroll's
original version of *Kindred.*

Kindred had opened at the Maxine Elliott Theatre
in New York on December 26, 1939, and closed in
mid-January 1940. The year 1940 was to mark another

Broadway failure for Carroll when *The Old Foolish-ness* opened in New York City on December 20, 1940, and closed after only three performances.

This drama's disappointing run must be attributed to the fact that Carroll did not follow the lesson he professed to have learned from the failure of *Kindred;* i.e., in the future to aim for "clarity and lucidity." Comments by the opening night critics on *The Old Foolishness* reflect Carroll's lack of success on this level. Brooks Atkinson spoke of the play being "nebulous in thought" and maintained that the mysticism of Carroll needed something as coherent and forceful as the church to give him power. Richard Watts noted that there was confusion in the play and remarked that Carroll's mysticism had become "soft" and "fuzzy."

Despite the New York critics' unanimous disapproval, the play possesses much poetry and warmth and is distinguished by some effective scenes. The play reads particularly well because the moments of meditation and reflection which reading provides enable one to absorb the mystical implications, the symbolism, and the allegorical meanings. Although not intended for such a purpose, the play makes a poetic and attractive closet drama.

The Old Foolishness, the action of which occurs in 1940, centers on the three Sheeran sons who are engaged in totally different activities. Peter Sheeran is a serious and hard-working bachelor of thirty-five who has run the family farm since the death of his father. Francis, the next oldest brother, is presently being sought by the police because of I.R.A. activities. Tim, the youngest member of the family and the most intellectual, spends most of his time reading and thinking and plans to become a teacher.

Tim observes that Francis is seeking "blood and iron," but that he himself longs for "somethin' that's all aflame—but has no name." Peter expects that Tim will find the rewarding elements in life that lack of time and family duties prevented him from discovering.

While the three brothers' characteristics are being established, the audience learns of the existence of Maeve McHugh, who lived with Francis until the police raided the house in Dublin where the lovers had been staying. Dan Dorian, a local carefree individualist, who knew Maeve before she ran off with Francis, lauds Maeve's beauty: "a girl she is that God only makes once in ten twirls o' the moon." Yet, at the same time, Dorian also remarks that Maeve "has no beauty at all. It's something you don't *see*. You—you *know* it."

When Maeve arrives at the Sheeran cottage to deliver a message from Francis, she is extremely weary, but there floats about her a strange, delicate charm. She discusses Francis, maintaining that he might have achieved greatness but that his bravery and thirst for danger became enmeshed "by the wrong thing, the wrong cause." Although Peter treats her with hostility because of her illicit affair with Francis, she perceives that he is a fine, rare spirit who possesses a spark and depth of which no one else is aware.

Maeve's relationship with Tim also turns dynamic. Intelligent and well-educated, she inspires him to continue and intensify his studies and scholarly interests. The impact Maeve makes on Tim is so remarkable that he declares his love for her, though she responds somewhat enigmatically: "Only love me as I love you. Anything else will bring you unhappiness. You—might be something." Peter upbraids Maeve for letting Tim fall in love with her and prophetically and symbolically declares: "There's something in you no man can stand out against."

Dan Dorian, who regards himself a descendant of the legendary Irish hero Finn, takes Maeve to a ruined castle on a mountaintop in Mourne where Finn was reputed to have lifted a chunk out of the mountain and hurled it high in the air as an act of indignation against the world's corruption. In a castle room lighted only with shafts of moonlight, Dorian, Maeve, and Tim speak of the period seventeen centuries ago when great heroes and ideas ruled in Ireland. We hear that Queen Maeve of the old Gaelic folktales is Maeve McHugh's grandmother and that Maeve seeks a return to the ancient days of Ireland's greatness. As Nora Fintry in *The White Steed* symbolized a modern Niam, Maeve symbolizes a modern Queen Maeve. Again, pronouncedly, appears the Irish heroic theme.

Later Peter comes to the castle and expresses his love for Maeve, who returns his ardor but becomes frightened and reluctant to leave the magical locale of the castle. She observes that her shortcomings and will-o-the-wisp nature would trouble him if they should marry. Maeve promises never to leave him, but her answer is inconclusive:

If I do it won't be my fault. It will be something
stronger than me.
Oh Peter there are wonderful moments when I can see
Francis in you—without his fierceness—when I can see
Dan without his foolishness—Tim without his weakness—
when I can see the *whole wide world in you*—without its
turning and tossing.

Tim recognizes that "Dan loves you—Peter loves you.
We all love you—and we are all beginning to hate each
other because we love you." Further complications
develop when Francis surprisingly reappears and claims
Maeve. Francis and Peter exchange blows until Maeve
decides to leave because she will bring them only unhappiness. Although she loves Peter the most, she cannot be happy and content under the present circumstances.

Maeve goes off with Dan Dorian, and he asserts:
"Nothing can hold her. She's not for the likes o' you.
She belongs to *Finn*. Me chariot will carry her away
to him—and he'll take her up and on—and on—and
never stop going." Her heavenward departure reveals
the final symbolic meaning. She is not the Cathleen
ni Houlihan of Yeats; she is rather the very ancient
Ireland in its golden age when heroic figures such
as Finn dominated the country. She symbolizes heroism,
courage, love, joy, imagination, fulfillment, and a society of godlike proportions free from the ills and deficiencies which beset the present.

Earlier in the play, Maeve had lamented that contemporary Ireland has become obsessed with the notion
of love as sin:

It's all that matters—the sin of love, the sin of flying

feet running from God. The other sins don't matter. . . .
Our God is the gun, our hell is England, our beauty
is the blood of our young men spilt on the roadway,
our skeleton in the cupboard is the farmer, who is un-
lettered enough to love the land and the birds and trees,
and our vomit, our filth is some poor devil like me,
who believes that racing blood must have a meaning
and that God doesn't live only in the hearts of stone and
fear but that he runs when we run, is hurt when we are
hurt and sobs when we sob.

As long as such conditions prevail in Ireland, the
country must be tragically fragmented. Neither the
clergy (represented by the Canon who condemns
Maeve), the soldiers and political rebels (represented
by Francis), the scholars and intellectuals (represented
by Tim), nor the hard-working men of the soil (represented by Peter) are able to unite under present circumstances and heal the divisions. Each group touches
upon one another only tangentially; there is no pure,
unified harmonious viewpoint—only hatred, misunder-
standing, and a deeply scarred and maimed country.
Maeve, representative of the spirit of Ireland of centuries ago, concludes that there is no present hope for
a tormented and basically loveless Ireland. As Maeve
departs, each of the brothers returns to his particular
vocation, and the country and its people continue on
in the same bleak manner. Dan Dorian, who carries
Maeve away in his chariot, serves as a modern Puck
or sprite, a menial servant of Finn. Throughout the
play he carries on in a wild, carefree manner, appre-
ciating love, beauty, and heroism, and constantly
mocking manifestations of opposite qualities. He—an
O'Casey-like figure—symbolizes the more admirable as-

pects of ancient Ireland before Puritanism and other
modern illnesses and distortions blighted the country.

The symbolic meanings and the special significance
of Maeve McHugh are not clearly perceived unless the
play is read. Several of the drama critics and appar-
ently most of the Broadway audience could not understand the powerful and mesmeristic fascination which
Maeve holds for the three brothers, and their reaction
to the play was understandable because Carroll blurred
the symbolism.

Furthermore, the symbolism and mysticism force
most of the characters to be mere abstractions. They
represent qualities and attitudinize certain motifs, but
all too often they do not convey flesh and blood
qualities. They seem to have been created more to
represent ideas than to exist as human beings in their
own right. Hence when the figures become symbols—
and it is not absolutely clear to an audience that has
not preread the play what the symbols sometimes stand
for—the drama's impact collapses. Be it noted, nevertheless, that although the play is a theatrical failure,
it contains much poetry and demonstrates Carroll's
gift for creating a genuine atmosphere. Especially
notable in this connection is the second scene in Act
Two, set in a ruined castle in the Mourne mountains.
Here we have a departure from Carroll's usual approach: he now writes a long, sustained, heavily poetic,
and romantic episode. As moonlight shifts and flickers,
depending on the movements of the clouds, an ethereal
haze descends over the characters and the locale, and
for a time everyone seems genuinely caught in the re-

mote past. (In effective use of lighting and colors to develop a special aura, this episode has affinities to the Dublin street scene that opens the final act of O'Casey's *Red Roses for Me*.) These mountains were frequented by Finn, and, as the scene develops, so rich and delicate is the craftsmanship that a legendary time appears to be existing again in the present. This exquisite scene convinces that Carroll could, if he had so wished, sustain a charming and delightful poetic romanticism even though his more natural bent was wedded to realism, satire, and humor.

IV

Since he had developed a fervid and abiding interest in drama from the period of his student days in Dublin, Carroll sought opportunities to arouse a similar enthusiasm in others. This impresario aspect of his career was first manifested when he and two friends founded a neighborhood theatre in Glasgow in 1933. Carroll and his colleagues decided to stage plays that were rarely if ever presented in Scotland. As a result of their efforts, such works as *Hedda Gabler* and *An Enemy of the People* were made available, and several plays by such diverse talents as O'Neill and Pirandello were produced for the first time in this part of Great Britain. Carroll also served as the "resident" playwright of a little theatre founded by Molly Urquhart in 1939 at Rutherglen. His own works, including one-acters and children's plays, were especially popular with audiences who frequented this theatre.

In 1934 Carroll became, with James Bridie and others, one of the founding directors of the Glasgow Citizens' Theatre and also served as an advisor on productions. The excellence, and box office appeal, of his

Shadow and Substance is credited with saving this theatre from ruin. As Winifred Bannister concludes in his book on James Bridie: "Thus was the new Scottish theatre put on its feet by an 'Abbey' playwright." *The White Steed* and *The Wise Have Not Spoken* were also exceedingly successful at the Citizens' Theatre. This theatre thrived and, among other accomplishments, gave an opportunity to Scottish playwrights, such as Joe Corrie and Robert MacLellan, to have their efforts produced. Revivals of famous plays, past and present, from all countries furnished additional variety and appeal.

Carroll's long residence in Scotland (he seems never to have suffered from being an Irish expatriate) and his concern for the theatre there prompted him to write three full-length plays on Scottish subjects. The first of these dramatic works, *The Strings, My Lord, Are False,* actually premiered at the Olympia Theatre in Dublin on March 16, 1942, and proved to be a "hit" in Ireland. When, however, the play appeared later the same year on Broadway, it received unfavorable dramatic notices and continued for only fifteen performances.

The events described in *The Strings, My Lord, Are False* occur during the devastating German air raids in western Scotland in 1941. Carroll himself had served as a member of one of the fire rescue squads when Clydeside was under attack and possessed an intimate knowledge of the happenings in this time of torment.

The play's four scenes take place in a bomb shelter fashioned from a church crypt and in the refuge room

of the church's presbytery in Port Monica, a steel town
on the Firth of Clyde. Canon Courteney, the clergyman in charge, is a sympathetic and understanding
rector and a secure, stabilizing force as many people
seek refuge from the bombing and from the general
chaos resulting from the raids. Hundreds are slaugh-
tered during the German attacks, and thousands of
people are left homeless.

The Canon emerges as the play's focal figure. He
has the opportunity to return to the complete safety of
a clerical living in his native Ireland, but he will not
desert the people he knows and serves in his parish.
His aged housekeeper believes that he should seek
safety in southern Ireland, among his own people; but
the Canon argues that there exists no real distinction
among people. Since the devastating and demoralizing
raids have commenced, the Canon has behaved with
herculean strength and Christ-like spirituality. He is a
fountainhead of inspiration and encouragement, of
faith and love.

He insists that one should not retreat from life,
that one should plunge into existence offering every
goodness that humanity requires. He maintains that all
evil will pass in time, that the future must improve
and that everything can be rebuilt by what is *"within"*
man, not with what is outside. The present period is
a Calvary for the people, but the common struggle
against totalitarian oppression is holy, and the demons
of hell who encourage tyranny and barbarism will be
eventually repulsed.

Under the anguishing strain of the air raids the

individuals involved demonstrate a wide variety of reactions, and we view several different types of characters. Communist Ted Bogle, for instance, will not
help "the system" in any manner but will assist "the
people" on any occasion. Louis Liebens, the Jewish
war veteran who has lost an arm as a result of the
fighting during the Dunkirk evacuation, does everything possible to aid anyone in distress. He sets up a
lighting system in the darker section of the crypt, builds
telephone communications, and later even helps with
the birth of a baby. Liebens expresses so much pes-
simism and ironic humor and utters so many com-
plaints that he becomes one of the most memorable
characters in the corpus of Carroll's work, furnishing
badly needed comic relief. When he is pestered by a
child who inquires about his arm, he snaps, "I left
Dunkirk in such a hurry that I forgot it, but it's being
sent on by registered post. Why don't you go away to
the hens and ducks in the country and leave me here
in peace with the bombs?" Liebens, whose fiancée has
been killed by the Germans, will not allow deplorable
conditions to defeat his instinct for life. Carroll uses
this figure to symbolize the continual tragedy of past
and present history found especially in wars and per-
secution. Liebens represents the wandering Jew, regarded as an "ageless warrior, tireless wayfarer, the
spiritual nomad" and illustrates the perpetual suffering, perseverance, and resiliency of mankind.

A seemingly endless number of characters appear
and reappear during what Joseph Holloway perceptively describes as "more a moving picture of events

during the bombing of Glasgow than a play in the ordinary sense." Sadie O'Neill, for example, has been a prostitute for several years, but after witnessing the suffering and carnage and noting the scarcity of medical attendants, she returns to her first profession—nursing —and courageously and competently delivers children who are born during the most terrifying and powerful attack launched by the Germans.

In Carroll's episodic approach to dramatic structure we learn intermittently about Sadie's character, and we are also presented with snatches of information about other figures like Jerry Hoare. Hoare, a local journalist, symbolizes the disenchanted intellectual who has lost faith in living and in people. Jerry is about to be arrested as a draft-dodger, although he holds no religious or pacifistic convictions. He simply refuses to take an interest in humanity until he is aroused by the death of the girl who had broken their engagement.

The play kaleidoscopically shifts from episode to episode. We view one character for a brief while, then switch to another, and soon on to a third; we return to the first character and learn more about him, then a bit more about the second figure, and so on until, through such snatches and bits, a total picture of each of the dramatis personae is grasped. But the constantly shifting focus causes a disjointed effect and also a too obtrusively sprawling structure.

Further, the characters are too obviously preachments: Warden Bill Randall, for instance, who strives to keep everything on an even keel. He directs rescue operations and behaves altruistically throughout the

drama until he learns that his fiancée Iris is pregnant
by a canteen worker who was recently killed. For a
time Randall refuses to forgive Iris, but as death and
maiming and general chaos continue, Randall adopts
one of the favorite exhortations of the Canon and declares: "Maybe this world of smashed and broken things
all around us is teaching us things. Maybe the secret
of life means the lifting-up of the fragments, and the
piecing of them together with faith, and the going
on. . . ." In effect the Canon's convictions form a
refrain: "The world is full of mended things. . . . A
life is never broken by one piece of idiocy." The play
demonstrates—too obviously for really first-rate drama
—that such a philosophy works.

The only figure in the play beyond redemption is
Councillor McPearkie. Politician and entrepreneur,
McPearkie engages in black market activities, sells food
from the Food Reserves illegally, and profiteers in
every shady fashion. When adequate evidence is finally
obtained to bring about the arrest of McPearkie for
his illicit activities, the Canon maintains that this development represents some retuning of the strings of
life. At the moment the dominating aspects are evil
and tragedy: the strings of existence are false, inhar-
monious, twisted. When the general courage shown
by the people and the words of his former beloved
reclaim Jerry Hoare to a purpose in life, when Bill
Randall agrees to rear Iris's illegitimate child, these
and similar signs show that "the strings are being
tuned" and that life can yet be bettered and goodness
reasserted.

Several sections of the play possess much emotional intensity, but as a whole this drama can not be rated a success. The large number and variety of characters who seek shelter from the air raids are distracting, and the drama frequently becomes diffuse and overcrowded. Episodes switch too abruptly and with too much rapidity to yield ideal artistic dramatic coherence. The Canon does help to serve as a unifying force, but even his presence seems to bring only a choppy and sporadic cohesion. And for all his kindness and generosity the Canon seems too perfect, too ideal, too free from human faults. He appears a far cry from such more earthbound and believable creations of Carroll's as Canon Matt Lavelle (*The White Steed*) and Canon McCooey (*The Wayward Saint*). The perennial writers' difficulty of creating a really believable saintly type appears to have thwarted Carroll in this portrait.

Not only is an aura of sentimentalism manifest frequently throughout the play, but several of the episodes are obviously melodramatic and artificial. A set, posed quality hovers about some of the scenes, and too many of the characters are stereotypes. The reactions of several figures seem most improbable; for instance, the reformation of Sadie O'Neill and even Bill Randall's decision to rear Iris's child appear a bit too hasty and contrived. It is unfortunate that Carroll's craftsmanship did not equal the scattered and panoramic material with which he was dealing, although it is perhaps fairer to remark that the nature of the material itself defies expert craftsmanship.

Carroll's next full length Scottish play, *Green Cars*

Go East (1947), demonstrates that although now choosing a smaller canvas, he was still too message conscious. Set in a Glasgow East End tenement area, this drama extols the virtues of generosity, selflessness, enduring courage, and persistent faith in human nature, and proved to be a hit both on the Scottish stage and on television. Schoolteacher Mary Lewis, who has "an infinite capacity for sacrifice," supports her shiftless father and mother and supplies the tuition money and encouragement to help her younger brother Bill obtain his university education.

As the play develops Mary valiantly endures difficulty after difficulty. The drinking and brawling habits of her father, Ted, and the parents' obsessive spending on household possessions they cannot afford place one financial burden after another upon her. Furthermore, her snobbish and more well-to-do fiancé, Johnnie Mc-Hardie, becomes discontented, and the couple decide to terminate their engagement. But all the travail Mary stoically bears is compensated for when Bill successfully completes his studies and another brother, Charlie, is saved from the life of a wastrel by obtaining a steady job in the printing trade. While the parents are beyond reclamation, the two brothers manage to achieve a purposeful existence.

When Johnnie McHardie's lawyer father embezzles two thousand pounds, Johnnie seeks out Mary again, thinking that she possesses some magic elixir that could be applied to his own family difficulty. Johnnie remarks: "I'm not used to pain like you. . . . When I was told the news, I—I felt lost, as if I were in a fog.

Then I saw a green car going East—going to where people can take blows on the face without thinking that pain is unnatural. The green car had a meaning for me. It meant—you."

Yet, as Mary points out, no sensible escapes exist and no dream solutions. There are no bright, shining, colorful elixirs in the eastern sky or elsewhere. Mary declares: "To me life has neither end—east or west. Life is just life, and I accept it. If it has a blow for me, well, I'll take it because I must: if it has a kiss for me, I'll take *it* too, I suppose because I want to. But in either case, always—on. That's the secret. You learn it, after the first few blows."

Except for the figure of Mary Lewis, Carroll appears to be more interested in propagating his stiff-upper-lip philosophy than in sounding out his characters. His undoubtedly inspiring and uplifting theme stressed to an inordinate degree drives the play into sentimentality and gives it a rather old-fashioned Victorian flavor. We are preached at in the most obvious manner. And a sermon is one thing: an effective play incorporating a message another.

While much time was spent in developing the character of Mary Lewis, she remains unconvincing and unreal. She suffers too much and submits too patiently. Moments occur when her self-sacrificing nature and her dogged perseverance are persuasive, but she is too unnecessarily mild, and at times almost saccharine. The other members of the Lewis family are stock figures who lack freshness and uniqueness of quality and presentation.

The conventionality of most of the characterization mingles with material which is essentially tepid and non-dramatic. While the slum setting is conveyed with much realism and a genuine feeling for the scene, and while Carroll's persistent denunciation of the dishonest practices of businessmen (in this instance the figure of Gongg, who sells products on credit to people who cannot manage to pay) compels attention, the general motif of quiet struggle and determined endurance further enervates the play. *Green Cars Go East* generally has a sleepy, tranquil quality which does not furnish sufficient dramatic interest.

Two other faults can be observed: At the beginning of Act 1, several of the tenement dwellers, particularly Murphy and Bert Purdie, engage in some humorous and beguiling dialogue; then these gossipy minor characters disappear almost completely. Granted that their principal function was to furnish background and a semi-humorous opening, they took on such reality and richness of invention that their reappearance would have been welcomed, and could have been properly included in other parts of the play to furnish variety and comic touches. At the end of *Green Cars Go East* a brief reference to Murphy occurs, but the very brevity and incidental quality of the reference serves to point up more vividly the fact that Carroll has missed an opportunity to enliven the play.

Another noticeable deficiency is Carroll's persistent tendency to overlabor points and to include dialogue that is essentially circular rather than progressive. As a result, too much of the conversation merely marks time, and many of the same comments and observations about the improvident and irresponsible habits of Mr. and Mrs. Lewis, for instance, are reiterated over and over. A more succinct, selective approach to the material could have produced a tighter, much more interest-arousing drama. To be sure, some of the episodes and several of the conversations are competently written, but a small-scale domestic drama of this nature requires a heightening and a tautness that *Green Cars Go East* most assuredly lacks.

Carroll essayed an ambitious subject in *Weep for Tomorrow* (1948), and again he used Scotland as his setting. The action of the play occurs in the village of St. Bride's, whose population has been declining continually as people move away to take jobs in the large industrial cities.

The drama immediately focuses on its central figure, Angus Skinner. Skinner, who serves as the schoolmaster as well as being the principal legal authority and unofficial mayor of the community, attempts to prevent the village from becoming a ghost town. He dreams of the day when the turbulent Gadach River, which flows through the hamlet, can be harnessed and the electric power derived therefrom used to enlarge the village and increase the potential of the neighboring valleys.

After Skinner and his plans have been introduced, the play proceeds rather leisurely to present the other important characters and significant details. The introductory exposition tends to be mechanical and long-winded: we learn too baldly that the basic income of the town is derived from work in Geordie Austin's

furniture factory and that, since this company is committed to craftsmanship as opposed to cheap mass production, it has limited financial potential. (If the factory should terminate its business, the school would be closed and the people transferred en masse to the industrial city of Dundee, a plan already recommended by the governing council of that part of Scotland.)

The first character conflict occurs when Mr. Dalziel, representing the council, comes to visit the community, and he and Skinner dispute the situation: Skinner emphasizing clean, fresh living in a green world while Dalziel thinks primarily of inefficiency and the wasting of public money. Skinner poses the crucial question of the play: why cannot "the insane depopulation of the countryside be stopped?"

Next, a potential hero is mechanically and too obviously introduced. Allan Graham, a famous engineer, returns to his boyhood home for a visit and is persuaded by Skinner to investigate the feasibility of harnessing the river.

Complications develop when a strike occurs at Austin's Furniture Factory. From this point on, dramatic intensity builds up and remains throughout most of the rest of the play. Austin fires Bill Craigie, a local Communist, from his job for causing insubordination and dissension. Craigie and his well-educated, almost masculine daughter Femina (also a zealous Communist) lead a strike of the factory workers and precipitate a crisis that threatens the town's very existence.

When Graham returns with government authority to see how the Gadach River can be controlled, hope for the continued existence of the village is restored. In this climate of optimism Austin agrees to the strikers' demands and his factory reopens.

This optimistic feeling comes to nought, however, when Graham reports that the only likely place to harness the Gadach is Eastwood Bend, and this would necessitate the flooding and submerging of St. Bride's. Angus Skinner is crushed. The people will now be transferred to a slum section in Dundee, and they will lose their roots and the other advantages of the pleasant rural area.

The play is allowed to end on a note of excessive sentimentality as Skinner and a drinking companion lament the tragedy they believe has taken place. Another indication that Carroll's thinking about this play was careless occurs when Femina is praised by Allan Graham near the end of the drama for her "grace, power, beauty, elegance, poise," when, actually, power remains the only one of these qualities she has demonstrated. Her behavior and appearance featured hooliganism, scrubby male garb and manners, and wild emotionalism, and since Graham's remark is not ironic, the inconsistency stands starkly.

Weep for Tomorrow is marred further by unnecessary material which frequently distracts from the main action. The same mistake observed in *The Strings, My Lord, Are False* recurs here. Too much essentially verbose and repetitious material appears. The play is overfurnished to an unwieldy degree. In addition, *Weep for Tomorrow* is so slanted in favor of its point of view that it assumes a too obviously didactic and propagandistic tone.

It must be admitted, nevertheless, that the character of the elderly dominie, Angus Skinner, is an impressive creation. Skinner demonstrates an abiding love for humanity and for those things he feels will best help people lead more satisfying lives. Although at times—especially near the end—he is portrayed with too much sentimentality, the core of a memorable figure shines undiminished. He demonstrates that in the present time of expediency, the "heroic example is [not] outmoded."

Despite this positive achievement in character penetration, Carroll witnessed the failure of *Weep for Tomorrow* when it was performed on the Scottish stage. Realizing, however, that this drama contained much unfulfilled potential and believing that he could make improvements by thoughtful revision, Carroll rewrote the play and entitled it *Goodbye to the Summer*. As yet unproduced, *Goodbye to the Summer* has just been published by Robert Hogan's Proscenium Press, and such ready availability of the text could properly make the play a standard repertory vehicle.

As was the identical case with *Kindred,* the revised text is a considerable improvement, and the material now formed into a compelling drama of the old rural areas threatened by urbanization and the concomitant ills such a development brings. *Goodbye to the Summer*'s opening is more poetic and more atmospheric than the material found at the beginning of *Weep for Tomorrow*. Reality is clearly established, but the nostalgic, picturesque element essential to Skinner's drama of a restored, thriving St. Bride's immediately becomes emphatic.

The overpacked nature of the earlier play is lessened considerably. Carroll has eliminated almost fifty pages of material. Immediately apparent is the fact that three scenes found in Act 1 of *Weep for Tomorrow* are omitted in the later version. In one episode two young farmers appear and dispute vehemently over their land boundaries while Skinner serves as judge and arbiter. In another episode of the first version the wife of the recently dead Jock Ramsay arrives and discusses his passing with Skinner. Skinner had drawn up Ramsay's will, and he agrees to come to the Ramsays and read its contents. Neither of these scenes appears in *Goodbye to the Summer;* but the essence of the material from these occurrences is briefly alluded to, and, thus, the purpose involved, which is to demonstrate how Skinner serves as the judicial and family heart of the community, is still effectively retained. Both scenes in their original form cluttered the play; now succinctness reigns. A third scene found in *Weep for Tomorrow* is omitted completely. This involved the local clergyman, Minister Melville, who converses with Skinner and then proceeds to give a talk to the schoolchildren. The deletion of this episode, which served only as an opportunity to attack the clergy, helps to concentrate the action.

Another change involves engineer Allan Graham's character, now much softened. We no longer hear about his being a corespondent in a divorce case, and Carroll obviously wishes him presented in a more objective and more favorable light so that the one-sided approach used in the first play will be more equally counterbalanced by the progressive, "down with the old and up with the new" attitudes with which Graham becomes associated.

The same attempt to soften antagonism toward modernists like Graham, Bill Craigie, and Femina, who care not at all whether St. Bride's survives, may be observed in the second act; three sections inimical to the progressives are omitted in *Goodbye to the Summer*. The unit which shows the hunger and deprivation caused by the strike, brought on by the intransigency and unreasonableness of Craigie and his daughter, is deleted. Also omitted are occurrences such as Skinner selling his old harmonium to obtain money to buy food for people left hungry by the strike. We do not now hear about Skinner dispensing food to the hungry when they gather in his yard. The omission of the "soup and lean jaws" material which was juxtaposed with Femina's fiery orations encouraging the strike's continuance vastly lessens a negative reaction against the Craigies. Removed also is the long scene involving the desire of some strikers to return to work in the furniture factory. The omission of this section, which demonstrated the viciousness and vindictiveness of the Craigies and the other strike supporters, has the result of making those on strike appear not to be enemies of order, tolerance, and sanity—as they had previously been represented. A third scene involving a violent encounter between the strikers and six housewives who want their husbands to return to work and a bitter physical battering between Femina and her sister Katherine has been eliminated, and this deletion also ren-

ders Femina and the strikers less monstrous and ob-
noxious. Femina's vitriolic and rabble-rousing dialogue
is still evident, but the audience dislikes her less because she is now not involved in threatening and pun-
ishing those opposed to the strike, beating Katherine,
etc. The omission of the above scenes makes the new
forces for urbanization seem more understandable and
logical, and all of the *excessive* sentimentality for the
old tranquil rural way of life has disappeared. Carroll
has given more balance to the two basic points of view.
As a result, *Goodbye to the Summer* avoids being a
sermon and a propaganda vehicle for time-honored existence. Although the author's sympathies are detect-
able, the inevitability of some change is recognized.

In the third act of *Goodbye to the Summer* Carroll
adds another touch to soften Femina's character and
to make her and the viewpoint she represents less
reprehensible. In *Weep for Tomorrow,* Femina, at one
point, shares a drink with Skinner; the two then quarrel
and she exits on a harsh note. But in the revision
Skinner asserts that no matter what happens, he will
feel more deeply about her than anyone else. She is
astounded by this sincere declaration and inquires why
he feels this way. He replies tenderly, "Because you're
my lost sheep . . ." This statement, so perceptively
apropos, does not alter Femina's views but wins her
sympathy and deepens our understanding of both rebel
and schoolmaster. This remark particularly epitomizes
Skinner's tolerance and the depth of humanity he
possesses.

The play raises several important economic and po-

litical and social issues. Can high-quality crafted products survive against a general decay in taste, or will
cheap, mass-produced merchandise predominate? Will
individual freedom and liberty be further compro-
mised? Skinner glorifies the value of freedom, but
Graham thinks Femina's Communist ideas may be
valid because the "world's crazy and it needs order at
almost any price." The tragedy of emigration of the
best young intellectual and scientific talent is also observed for, as Dalziel says, "There is our Scottish tragedy . . . the export of our brains." But again the drain-
ing away of talent occurs in many other countries, so
that this problem, as well as the others, has universal
dimensions. Further, Carroll deals probingly with the
qualities of love, faith, and humanity versus everything
that is "ruthless, conscienceless and amoral."

Goodbye to the Summer is a most effective statement
of the tragedy of the passing of the old rural ways, a
sort of modern dramatic version of Goldsmith's *The
Deserted Village*. The summer of the past vanishes
and a new, harsher urban winter descends, but since
Carroll here controls the materials more objectively,
maudlin excesses are checked by the relentless march
of change. *Goodbye to the Summer,* in fact, is the most
expert appraisal of its main theme in modern drama,
and the play deserves attention, which its recent pub-
lication should induce. Furthermore, it is by far the
best of Carroll's Scottish plays.

V

While the 1940s might well be considered as Carroll's Scottish drama period, he did create one rather effective serious Irish play during this decade. *The Wise Have Not Spoken,* written in 1942 and produced at the Abbey Theatre in 1944 and in London in 1946, bears an essential thematic resemblance to one of the issues raised both in *Weep for Tomorrow* and, later, in *Goodbye to the Summer.* The various social and economic problems faced by Ireland in the World War II period can be solved, the silenced priest Tiffany argues, by "love, dignity, an understanding of each other, a supernatural meeting-point as old as time, . . ." On the other hand, the embittered Francis Mac-Elroy calls for a Communist revolution brought about by social upheaval and blood. The play's structure stresses these opposing viewpoints, but in a generally slack and slow-paced manner.

It is evident at once that the introductory explication lacks economy. Too much background explication must be presented before the drama can reach points of intensity, and the presentation is long-winded. As the plot begins we learn that the MacElroy farm is to be sold at auction despite the hard-working efforts of Peter, Francis's brother. This farm, like many others, needs money for additional seed and machinery and to pay workers' salaries. Because of such difficulties, several farms are being vacated, and the laborers are leaving the country to seek work elsewhere.

Besides the economic deficiencies of the time, Ireland is beset by an excessive number of civil service employees, narrow clerical views, Puritanism, intellectual snobbism, and unscrupulous commercial interests. These aspects not only prevent the nation from realizing its potential but also bring frustration and apathy to thousands of people.

The long exposition continues as the audience hears that Tiffany had at one time attempted to organize the local farmers into a cooperative association and urged them to purchase a former aristocratic estate consisting of 500 acres of productive land. Through much self-sacrifice, the farmers' union and Tiffany managed to offer a more than reasonable price for this property, which could have been turned into a successful business venture that would have given the local farmers a secure opportunity to thrive and prosper. But the land was auctioned to a religious community of Spanish monks. Carroll is shaping his material to indict both Church and State. The property in question would have helped the destitute and given prosperity to the area; this potentiality outweighed the claims of the monks. The Irish state, too, was delinquent in not trying to help its own people first; again outsiders from

another country had more influence than the needy
natives.

As a result of this continued activity on behalf of
the farmers, Father Tiffany has been officially silenced
by the church and is no longer a priest in good standing. He now works as an ordinary laborer on the Mac-
Elroy farm and leads an extremely humble existence.
Acutely aware of the country's faults, Tiffany, much
later in the play, puts his hand on the heart of the
issue when he asserts that freedom from England has

> not given us greater sanctity, greater dignity, greater
> understanding of each other. It has given us instead
> swarms of unnecessary state-paid humbugs: a new class
> of insufferable Gaelic snobs: and a young priesthood who
> run motor-cars and the Gaelic Athletic Association for
> the greater glory of God. We have even invited to Ireland
> that historical alien the Puritan, with all his cruelties
> and negations.

Tiffany is just as much aware of the deficiencies and
failures of Ireland as is the Communistic Francis Mac-
Elroy. But whereas MacElroy offers "blood and steel,"
"laws and edicts," Tiffany does not believe that any
government can really cope with inherent economic
and social injustices found to a greater or lesser degree
in every country. Unlike Francis, who believes in even-
tual perfection and mass utopianism, Tiffany urges a
deeper and genuine morality and spiritual conscious-
ness.

For the purpose of tightening the structure and
heightening the play's impact, this conflict should have
been more sharply presented right at the beginning
with the later incorporation of some additional back-

ground material which now causes the initial act to drag. A striking opening could have easily been achieved because Francis MacElroy, who limps heavily as a result of a war wound incurred while fighting against Franco's forces in the Spanish Civil War, is confirmed in the way of blood. The economic and social difficulties of Ireland gall him—the fact that thousands of his countrymen must migrate yearly in order to find work, the fact that most of the land is owned by banks and similar powerful financial interests, the fact that at least 20,000 people in Dublin subsist on a mere sixpence a day. Francis is willing to fight and die to change the system, and he sees the spilling of blood as the only hope.

Juxtaposed between the two views of Francis and Tiffany is staunch and hardworking Una MacElroy. She respects both Tiffany and her brother, although the latter is extremely difficult to satisfy and to live with. Una has an opportunity to avoid the hardships found in rural Ireland by marrying schoolteacher Martin Langley, a young, pompous Gaelic enthusiast. When Langley reneges on his promise to marry Una, we witness symbolically how the "state-paid humbugs" and "insufferable Gaelic snobs" that Tiffany had earlier decried refuse attempts to improve and unify the country. Una is a symbolic representation of a better Ireland brought to truth, harmony, and enlightenment. When Tiffany attempts to persuade Martin Langley to marry the long-suffering Una, he observes that Una would "redeem" the schoolmaster from his faults and shortcomings.

Meanwhile Peter MacElroy is forced to quit the

farm and take a job in Glasgow—another example of depopulation and the loss of a sincere, hard-working, self-sacrificing type which the country so desperately requires. When the moment comes for the bank representatives to auction the MacElroy farm, Francis determines to resist by physical force. He unthinkingly brushes aside Tiffany's question as to whether people can "live with the ideals" they die for, his thoughts turning only on the absolute necessity for a Communist republic. Tiffany forcefully insists that the republic Christ envisaged is more important, the end of Francis's Communist utopia being "iron and stone," while the end of Tiffany's concept is "the Vision Beautiful." But both goals are thwarted in Ireland for as Tiffany concludes, "We are all too lazy for yours—and all too mean for mine."

When Francis attempts to defend the farmhouse from foreclosure by force, Una (as Ireland) cannot leave, and neither will Tiffany, since spiritual depth can never completely desert the country. Francis is killed in the ensuing gunfight while the innocent Tiffany, caught in the line of fire, also meets death, mumbling "the good and the evil . . . the foolish and the wise . . . they must mingle." Tragically, Una remains isolated and alone, repeating the words that Tiffany has just uttered. If Ireland is now to improve, militancy must be put aside, and spirituality and genuine brotherhood must predominate.

The Wise Have Not Spoken is a generally tense, engrossing, and suspenseful play. It advocates a generous humanity of love expressed in the three Scottish plays and in most of Carroll's earlier Irish subject matter. Reminiscences especially of *The Old Foolishness* occur. Both Maeve in the latter drama and Una in the present play represent Ireland in its more ideal possibilities—a country that could obtain desirable virtues and stable family qualities although, at present, intellectual, spiritual, economic, and militant currents stir the scene into an often frenzied whirlpool. Above all, Ireland must reject violence. (Tiffany's refusal to condone arms is similar to the reason Maeve rejected the gunman brother in *The Old Foolishness*.)

Carroll's own philosophy is expressed through the various statements and speeches of Tiffany. Yet Carroll succeeds in balancing the opposing viewpoints by presenting Francis MacElroy as an understandable and not unlikable character. Francis's compassion for Una and the kindly deed he performs for his brother Peter increase respect and sympathy, so that although Carroll does not favor his theories, he avoids conceiving of and handling Francis as a straw man. Believable, vibrant, intense, Francis is a realized character of flesh and blood. Comprehensible, too, is Tiffany's shrewd and perceptive observation that "One little twist of the mind twenty years ago in a schoolroom would have made Francis a great Jesuit." He certainly stands as one of the most credible portraits of an Irish revolutionary to be found in contemporary drama, and it is a measure of Carroll's success that an audience can sympathize with Francis and his views without having to accept them.

The faults of *The Wise Have Not Spoken* are secondary in relation to the success of its theme and its characterizations. Nevertheless, quite apparent is the fact that Carroll, as he did especially in *The Strings, My Lord, Are False,* has brought in too many characters and employed too wide a canvas. The presence of farm laborer Paddy Ardee can be justified on the basis of comic relief, but the scenes involving the demented Catherine (a type of Ophelia), while never dull, ultimately distract. Catherine, who eventually has to be certified and taken to an asylum because of her feelings of guilt about an illicit love affair, symbolizes overscrupulosity and an unhealthy Puritanism which plagues Ireland. Some of the other supernumeraries, such as Andy Redfern who represents the unscrupulous gombeen man type, and the old rebel Mulligan, who has sold out to the system, also clutter the scene. If the play had concentrated on Peter, Francis, Una, and Tiffany and omitted Catherine, Martin Langley, and Redfern, Carroll would not have conveyed as many symbolic themes, but he would have produced a more realistic play since one tends to agree with T. C. Murray's observation, quoted by Joseph Holloway: "What a County Louth household! It was too much to expect that so much misfortune could be crowded together under one roof."

Also noticeable in the American premiere of the play, well acted at the Off-Broadway Cherry Lane Theatre in February 1954, was the realization that Carroll had once again been too obviously didactic. The tendency to sermonize and preach unduly at times, especially in Tiffany's role, strikes the audience as one of the features of the play that could have been lessened without any weakening of the thematic motifs. Carroll himself was later to admit that he lectured too much in the play and blamed this tendency on the fact that the play was written during the war when, as he remarked, "hearts broke easily and the dawns were all tragically flame-lit."

All in all, the play's virtues outweigh its faults. The dialogue lilts and stings and continually captures attention, and the play lingers long in the memory after it has been witnessed. Moreover, *The Wise Have Not Yet Spoken* possesses a vitality and universality in the confrontations between Tiffany and Francis MacElroy that epitomize two opposing points of view toward life forcefully and clearly.

In addition to his work in the drama, Carroll wrote numerous short stories throughout his lifetime. But Carroll's main concern was the theatre, and he admitted to friends that his short stories were written mainly as an avocation with entertainment as their fundamental goal. It is apparent from the stories themselves that Carroll enjoyed writing them since they are, in general, dominated by a mood of zestfulness and beguiling delight.

Typical of Carroll's work in this genre is "Me Da Went Off the Bottle." The narrative involves the Grady family whose breadwinner is a likable and kindly individual when he takes a few drinks, but when completely sober, turns into a nagging, unpleasant martinet who makes his wife and children edgy and unhappy. When a new priest comes into the parish and determines to wage an attack on drinking, he selects Mr. Grady and eleven other family men in the area to be his principal crusaders against Bacchus. Indeed, he goes so far as to denominate his choices the twelve apostles and to designate Mr. Grady as St. Peter. From then on the children are constantly spanked and browbeaten, and general tyranny pervades the household. But eventually St. Peter falls from grace, returns to the bottle, and he and the family once again resume normal humanity as the "land became sweeter from the human foibles of the people who toiled it."

While many of Carroll's stories are written in this vein of sheer good-natured humor, he also essayed stories that showed other facets of the Irish character. In "She Went by Gently," for example, he examines the deeply religious beliefs of an Irish midwife who travels miles to deliver an illegitimate child. The midwife manages to baptize the infant before it passes away. Although the child dies, the midwife cannot feel that the event was tragic because of her conviction that baptism has saved his soul and brought him safely to heaven. In "Dark Glory" a former jockey named Martyn Cliffe suffers continual distress and torment because he once accepted a bribe which prevented the race's favorite from winning. Since Cliffe's principal interest in life involved the love of fine horses, his remorse is more intense because he believes he has wronged the horse itself.

In several of his stories Carroll turns to the ghostly and mystery type in which he is able to build considerable suspense. "My Learned Friend, Hogan" deals with a murder which at first is thought to be an accident. By convincing the suspected murderer that the missing corpse has returned for vengeance, a clever accountant solves the mystery of the killing and brings the perpetrator to a violent reckoning. An emphasis on mysterious intuitions between lovers and between members of a wild family of sailors becomes the basis for most of the narrative interest generated in "The Virgin and the Woman." Though he is hundreds of miles away and on land, the elderly John Marron is able to imagine his son Andrew attempting to control a ship in a ferocious storm. So close have father and son been in their thoughts and feelings that Marron dies from tension at the very moment that Andrew's ship sinks.

The majority of Carroll's stories can be classified as tales of humor, character sketches, and ghostly sagas— all of which usually inculcate some moral point, sometimes too obtrusively, at other times with just the precise amount of understatement and subtlety. Rarely does he venture to write the type of short story which is intended to be read and reread for additional insights and perceptions. When he does attempt such a purpose, as in "Home Sweet Home," his most artistic narrative, he demonstrates an ability to handle his material skillfully. "Home Sweet Home" centers on a sensitive and unhappily married middle-aged man. Martin, the protagonist, decides to leave his home and desert his wife, but he learns from a tramp that such an action is too late; he is already branded too deeply by his wife to be free. The branding is now indelible, so he must return home and continue to endure unhappiness. The tramp, or Thread Man, as he is called in the area, suffers a similar burden. He too observes the ambivalence of a home—a necessity but frequently an evil, a place of ill comfort, a kind of desired but undesirable trap. The tramp looks forward to a future millennium when homes may be done away with, since he regards them as "the cruelest of all things on earth."

"Home Sweet Home" lingers long in the memory and repays endless readings. It stirs thoughts of man's deepest instincts, of love-hate relationships, and of the perpetual conflict between his need to be free and the demands of conformity, between man's highest aspirations and earthbound requirements.

Carroll's short stories are generally credible in plot and are marked by a deft handling of dialogue and local color. He captures fully the flavor and atmosphere of the scene about which he writes, sustains narrative interest, and with relatively few strokes, brings his characters to life. His narratives never fail to be entertaining. On the other hand they lack symbolic depths and, except for "Home Sweet Home," the intriguing interplay of memories, reflections, and internal perceptions which are the hallmarks of the best modern short stories.

The stories do illustrate many of the elements found in Carroll's plays: his gift for humor, satire, and irony; his talent for character revelation and inventive plotting; and his fundamental moral concerns. The preachment aspect basic in many of the narratives is reminiscent of Carroll's early playwriting while the more amusing tales link closely with the later period when his reforming zeal decreased but never completely vanished.

VI

The Devil Came from Dublin (1951) —earlier entitled, in somewhat different versions, *Chuckeyhead Story* (1950) and then *Border Be Damned* (1951) — marked a new phase of Carroll's career. Writing about a subsequent play similar to *The Devil,* Carroll noted that his earliest efforts had been produced with "a bee in my Irish bonnet about reforming people through the medium of the stage." At present, his emphasis was upon merriment. He now rejected the notion of instilling reforming ideas and turned to writing satirical romps. Of *The Devil,* as of the subsequent *The Wayward Saint,* Carroll could well remark: "I have no axes to grind. I just want people to enjoy themselves and stop lifting the lids off the Carroll philosophical dustbins in search of alleged truth."

The Devil Came from Dublin, eventually published in 1958 in a somewhat revised form, demonstrates Carroll's ability to create wild rollicking comedy. This play proved to be extremely popular with Dublin and London audiences, although it never reached Broadway. (It was shown in the United States in 1962 as part of the University of Rochester Modern Irish Drama Festival.) The setting of this romp, called a "satirical extravaganza," is the village of Chuckeyhead, a hamlet located on the Free State side of the Ulster border. During the World War II period the people of Chuckeyhead engaged in smuggling every imaginable commodity and product into Northern Ireland. The whole town subsists on smuggling activities and the profitable business resulting therefrom.

This situation provides a rich vein of humor: one smuggler conceals a hundred valuable watches in his grandmother's coffin; another pretends that he is deaf and dumb as he stands with his mouth full of gold rings while the Customs Officer examines his belongings. And much amusement results from the constant denigration of the anti-smuggling law itself: how "do you expect dacent men like ourselves to work within the law?" is a question that frequently recurs. It is the law that is made to seem the fool while the people outwit it at every turn.

The most crucial challenge to the activities of the Chuckeyheadonians occurs when an eminent Dublin barrister, Udolphus McCluskey, is appointed by the government to be the new District Judge to suppress thoroughly the notorious smuggling activities in the area. McCluskey is a pompous, snobbish teetotaler who is fond of drinking tomato juice and appears utterly incorruptible. The townspeople set out to reform McCluskey. He is regarded as the devil who must be de-Puritanized and reeducated in "the dacent human and Christian weaknesses." The townsfolk attempt to influence him to become one of themselves by, among other things, convincing him that the border is an English crime.

This topsy-turvy approach to the characters and the material adds immeasurably to the general merriment. Almost everyone in Chuckeyhead is a consummate liar, and much comedy is extracted from their fantastic fabrications, double meanings, and tongue-in-cheek tomfoolery. For most of the play Udolphus McCluskey is kept continually off-balance. When, for example, he asks for innkeeper Stanislaus Brannigan's close cooperation to help him discover and root out the smugglers, Brannigan, who is one of the chief miscreants, replies, "Your honour can count on me to keep a watchful eye on you every hour of the day and night." Brannigan then proceeds with a delicious denunciation of smuggling in which he piles numerous lies, exaggerations, and ironies one atop the other.

The enjoyable dialogue is reinforced by a wild and somewhat improbable set of characters. There is a middle-aged Sergeant of the Guards, who produces maudlin verse when he has drunk a bit too heavily; a usually inebriated Customs Officer who works with the smugglers and is in danger of losing his job when he's sober since he claims to be efficient only when he's drunk; and a general assortment of amusing tricksters.

The most diverting character in the play is the youthful Rita Ronan, who is a direct descendant of Synge's Pegeen, the barmaid in *The Playboy of the Western World*. The handsome and nubile Rita possesses an incurable romantic strain—she reiterates that she will marry only a hero. Nominally, she is the girl-friend of Mike MacNamara, the leader of the smug-glers. Rita regards the arrival of the new Deputy Jus-tice as a heroic challenge for MacNamara. She becomes ecstatic over the new danger faced by Mike—she be-lieves he has a chance to become another Nero, Crom-well, or Napoleon. If Mike is caught and imprisoned, she would be happy to behold him suffering in jail, delighted to see him in chains. If he should be jailed and then escape, she would revel in the glory of his being a hunted felon. She is infuriated when Mike re-fuses to go to jail after being discovered by Udolphus.

For a time Rita builds up Udolphus as her real hero. She pictures him severe and incorrupt on the judicial bench delivering stern justice and punishment, undeterred by unpopularity or threats to his life, a hero who can not be bribed for any price. She even requests that she be sentenced to jail so that she can experience the power of his stern control: "sentence me to jail," she exclaims, "till I get the thrill of it."

Rita has so overly romanticized the whole situation that she keeps calling the smugglers' activities "the cause" and regards them with doting eyes as the "last of the rebel breed." Even when the play ends happily, Rita cannot be content with the love of Mike Mac-Namara, but must be solaced by the thought—obviously borrowed from Shaw's *Man and Superman*—that she can be the mother of a son who will be lion-like and abolish the border. She can then be the mother of a hero.

For sheer high-spirited satire on the romantic illu-

sions and fantasies that pass through the minds of many
Irish, the Rita Ronan material is comic exaggeration
carried to its illogical logical heights. Even such incidental touches as allusions to Rita's former English
admirer who threw himself off a bridge because of un-
requited love but landed safely in a muddy, swampy
area add superlatively to the total effect of romantic
fooling.

Many of the play's antics are, of course, mere farce,
but it is inspired farce, gifted fooling, with a generous
display of wit, humor, and sheer good spirits. George
Jean Nathan found the drama "jolly, intelligent, and
warming" with a "healthy undercurrent of whimsical
sagacity." The wild improbability of many of the play's
happenings illustrates anew Carroll's powers of invention and imagination and his far-above-the-average
talent for satiric observation and irony. In this play
Carroll successfully blends some high comedy material
with the more farce-like strokes derived from broadly
humorous situations. *The Devil Came From Dublin*
emphasizes low comedy, while its successor, *The Wayward Saint,* contains more of the elements of high
comedy. Carroll demonstrates that his talent can be-
stride both forms. If he had wanted to devote his dramatic career to comedy, he could unquestionably have
written highly popular and entertaining plays in this
genre.

But never is Carroll far away from serious moral
points, which in *The Devil* are turned to satire. Particularly striking is the observation that if smuggling
in Chuckeyhead were abolished, the people would be

destitute or forced to migrate because no other work
is available. Under the surface Carroll can not forget
serious questions.

Yet in his two satirical comedies the technique is so
light-hearted and wry that never does the moralizing
distractingly intrude. *The Devil Came from Dublin*
makes its points about the overly romantic qualities
in the Irish nature, the deficiencies of Puritan rigor,
and an overlegalistic preoccupation with non-essentials,
and the need for decent men rather than just good
men. But these didactic elements are graciously em-
bedded in a happy context.

Notable too is the fact that Carroll improved this
play by revision. The original version of *The Devil
Came from Dublin,* entitled *Chuckeyhead Story,* contained several weaknesses. The play commenced with
an unduly slow exposition about the border division
between Ulster and the Republic and did not fully develop the madcap possibilities of Rita Ronan. In the
final version Rita is no longer a schoolmistress, but
rather a wildly daring lady of independent means, full
of fun, mischief, and romantic fantasies. Her romanticism is much more exaggerated in the final revision
and thus becomes three-dimensional and far more
amusing.

The *Chuckeyhead Story* also suffered by being un-
humorously talky in various sections and by being, at
times, too serious and moralistic. There were remarks
about Udolphus McCluskey's "small man's spite" of
enjoyment from a drop of brandy in tomato juice and
an overly emphasized animosity on the part of the

people who objected to McCluskey's prosecution of the smugglers. Such serious and biting qualities lessened the play's bonhomie and darkened the beguiling comic tone.

In the revision, Carroll has wisely developed the amusing figure of Customs Officer Ignatius Farrell (only mentioned in the original play) so that he lends a considerable variety of comedy, most of which flows from his affinity for the bottle. While the role of Farrell has been broadened, the figure of the "unbalanced aviator," Joe Murnaghan, who appeared in the original version of the play, has been deleted. Murnaghan, who enjoyed flying about the countryside, served as an almost pointless distraction in the first script, his function being to keep the Irish love of adventure in our minds and to give Rita Ronan a possible alternative to Mike; but the increased attention given to Rita and a more pointed concentration on her relations with Udolphus and Mike eliminate the need for the incredible aviator.

The ending of the final version is much more succinct and forceful, emphasis being placed on a son of Rita's and Mike's who will ultimately abolish the border. The conclusion, in comparison with the ending of *Chuckeyhead Story* when the smugglers' group merely stood in silence to honor the memory of Udolphus, is more memorable and more in keeping with the lively and sportive tone of the play.

Although a satirical fantasy rather than a satirical extravaganza, *The Wayward Saint* (1955) follows the carefree humorous vein inaugurated by *The Devil Came from Dublin.* In some ways it is an even more delightful romp than the previous comedy. The good humor and whimsy of *The Wayward Saint* establishes itself immediately, and this mood of joy and pleasantness pervades the three acts. Consistently inventive, imaginative, and amusing, the play is composed of one good-humored stroke after another.

The opening introduces a delectably entertaining situation. Canon Daniel McCooey has been transferred to a remote rural parish because of his St. Francis of Assisi like capering with animals and rumors of miracles and visions associated with his activities. McCooey is popularly rumored to be a saint, but as the Bishop of Oriel declares, "Saints are confounded nuisances and I just won't have them in my diocese."

This remark typifies the quaintness, satire, and charming irony of the play. When the Baron Nicholas de Balbus, an emissary of the devil, appears, we are treated to more of the same light-hearted whimsy. The Baron complains about the tastelessness of Irish food and the vagaries of Irish weather, which intensifies his rheumatism. He voices his disappointment with his assignment to Ireland; he had especially opted for "America where they don't even believe we exist."

The Baron's mission is to ensnare McCooey, whose kindly virtues if corrupted would furnish the infernal powers with a triumphant conquest. The Baron attempts to work on the vanity of the Canon and convince him that he really is a saint. The devil's representative also intends to corrupt everyone associated with the Canon, especially his staid, middle-aged housekeeper, Miss Killicat.

As the play develops Baron de Balbus has considerable success in accomplishing his goals. The Baron's
vocal blandishments and such specific acts as regaining
the Canon's two pet donkeys stir the parish priest's
dormant vanity, and he begins to think that he is a
saint after all. Meanwhile Miss Killicat lets down her
hair, dresses more prettily, and thinks seriously of following the Baron's suggestion of changing her name
from Mary Anne to Desiree. She even gains first place
over the much younger Maura Monigan in the contest
to marry grocer Martyn McDara who, although he is
"a mean dried-up little spider," is eagerly sought because "He's a man, Canon, and this is Ireland."

Carroll adds a further amusing element when he al-
lows the Baron to be unduly charmed by the Canon.
A special messenger has to be sent to earth to caution
the Baron and to warn him that Satan himself believes that the Baron is "growing much too fond of
the victim!" To which the Baron retorts, "Damn it all
I just can't help it. The old boy is irresistible." Threats
of dire punishment, however, return Nicholas de Balbus to his delegated duties.

The Canon's love of animals continually influences
his activities: when a lion escapes from a travelling
circus, Carroll brings in another diverting plot twist
in which—as in the Androcles saga—the Canon and the
lion become immediate friends. This relationship opens
an additional area of humor as the lion takes an immediate dislike for the Bishop and amusingly intimidates
the latter.

When it appears that the devil will win the soul of

Canon McCooey, the innocence and humility of Maura
Monigan and her prayers manage to save him. Although Carroll is still implying a moral, the point is
made so gracefully and naturally in the context that it
passes smoothly as a credible part of the play.

The play is truly a delight in its genre. Not only
continually merry and gaily colored entertainment, it
is also well crafted, with clever plot twists and happenings appropriate to a simple rural setting. No excess
verbiage or drawn-out dialogue mars its smiling surface. As one of the Broadway first-night audience who
saw this play, the present writer was delighted with its
wit and humor. The play was obviously not a full scale
comic masterpiece since much of its material tends to be
whimsically slight and several of the humorous effects
depend on exceptionally competent acting. Nevertheless, *The Wayward Saint* seemed to contain all the in-
gredients and talents needed for a long run except for
the curiously awkward performance of Paul Lukas as
Baron de Balbus. For some reason Lukas appeared to
be sleepwalking or even ill. He said his lines matter-
of-factly and derived only a small part of the humor
inherent in his role. While the other parts were acted
to perfection, Lukas appeared to be almost a saddened
undertaker participating unenthusiastically and completely out of place in a wild revelry. The strange case
of Lukas was commented on by several critics. Brooks
Atkinson, for example, found *The Wayward Saint* "en-
chanting" and praised its "gaiety, sweetness, innocence
and grace of spirit," but he observed that Lukas occasionally spoke unintelligibly, that his acting was un-

sure, and that his indifferent performance had the effect of blurring some of the play's contrast. Carroll himself complained in *Variety* that he had "lost" a good play on Broadway because of the miscasting of Lukas.

Several years later when I wrote to Carroll about this production, he responded that Lukas had seriously injured the play and had "refused my many requests to resign as he had a 'run of the play' contract." Thus a play that needed an actor such as Cyril Ritchard or Rex Harrison in the role of the Baron was limited to a three-week Broadway engagement principally because of some lethargic and erratic acting in a very important role.

It is of interest to note that *The Wayward Saint* has been a favorite of the German State Theatre for many years in an excellent translation by Elisabeth Freindlich of Vienna. In a letter to me Carroll declared, "The Germans are very attached to it. This year [1968], the famous German composer, Mark Lothar, with my permission, turned it in German into a light opera. At their request I flew to Munich where it had its premiere at the State Theatre. An amazing night of songs and music—15 curtains, and the Munich audience just wouldn't go home! Have never experienced such a premiere even on Broadway. The play is now in the repertoire of the State Theatre there, and I hope it remains there, as Mark Lothar did a wonderful job on the adaptation. . . . For some reason which I can't fathom, the Germans like my plays even as much as the Americans did."

One of the most unfortunate occurrences connected

with Carroll's career was that the American production of *The Wayward Saint*—as humorous and as imaginative a fantasy in its own way as O'Casey's *Cock-A-Doodle Dandy,* though not as poetic and as lyrical—did not have better casting in the vital role of Baron Nicholas de Balbus.

After *The Devil Came from Dublin* and *The Wayward Saint* were produced, Carroll's dramatic work was virtually ended. He did complete the fine revised *Goodbye to the Summer* and took the manuscript of an early unpublished and unproduced play about Jonathan Swift, revised it thoroughly, and had the satisfaction of seeing it appear successfully on B.B.C. television in 1956 and later published in 1966. Several of the scenes of this work—*Farewell to Greatness*—have power and vigor. There are some excellent passages involving the relationship between Swift and Stella, and the final scene, when the deranged Dean orders the bell of his cathedral to be tolled in funeral cadence on the anniversary of his birth, teems with intensity. But most of the encounters between Swift and Vanessa are too melodramatic, although Carroll's theory that Vanessa was the seducer illuminates somewhat Swift's Puritanical attitudes and behavior. But if *Farewell to Greatness* has a circular motion, and its structure is too choppy and episodic to be truly effective on stage, nevertheless, Carroll has captured the essentially ambivalent and enigmatic nature of the Dean of St. Patrick's.

In his final years Carroll retired from active work because of poor health. He died quietly from a heart seizure on October 20, 1968, at his home in Bromley, Kent, to which he had moved from Scotland in the 1940s.

Any overall estimate of Carroll's career must indicate that he well deserves a permanent place in contemporary Irish and English drama with his two finest achievements (*Shadow and Substance* and *The White Steed*), with two highly enjoyable satirical comedies (*The Devil Came from Dublin* and *The Wayward Saint*), and with three plays which have faults but which are talented works (*Things That Are Caesar's, The Wise Have Not Spoken,* and *Goodbye to the Summer*). In addition, Carroll has created the most convincing portraits of clergymen and clerical life yet to appear on the Irish stage. As one critic has noted, Carroll "has neither peer nor imitator in this kind of Irish play." Since the clergy enjoy such a dominant role in the life of the people, in-depth portrayals of their character and activities are fundamental in understanding Ireland. In the enthusiasm for the accuracy of such portraits as Canon Skerritt, Canon Lavelle, Father Shaughnessy, and curates like Fathers Kirwan and Corr, it should not be forgotten that Carroll has created memorable characters from all walks of life. O'Flingsley, Julia Hardy, Angus Skinner, Louis Liebens, Francis MacElroy—to mention just a sampling—are here representative.

At his best Carroll is one of the wittiest and talented masters of dramatic satire and irony twentieth century drama has produced. Although his two non-reforming extravaganzas abound in humor and ironies, he demonstrated a born genius for these qualities throughout most of his career. Quite central to his work was his realization that at heart the Irish character is filled with mysticism. Carroll once said that an Irishman "knows he is the lost child of some celestial hall of high splendors." He wrote that deep spiritual stirrings are inherent in the Irish nature and quoted AE's line, "You cannot all disguise the majesty of fallen gods." When Micheal MacLiammoir wrote about Irish mystical drama, which involved a "strange war between Paganism and Christianity . . . that has obsessed a considerable portion of Irish thought since Oisin argued with Patrick," he traced its origins to Yeats's *The Land of Heart's Desire,* but he noted that Carroll's *Shadow and Substance* particularly reflected this issue in its presentation of Brigid who, MacLiammoir argues, has mixed a great Celtic goddess of pagan antiquity with the Christian St. Brigid:

> They are two figures, it is true, but so interwoven, so beautifully entwined, that they have become as one in the imagination, whether the process of their merging has been conscious or no. . . . A girl like Mr. Carroll's Brigid is the perfect type in which to hear the honied, luring voices of the pagan world, and how easily she might mistake them for the voices of the authentically blest—that is, to me, one of the chief motives in *Shadow and Substance.*

This quality, already observed in *The White Steed,* gives most of Carroll's plays a universality and depth lacking in less thoughtful and perceptive Irish writers and further increases the lure his work holds.

With all his accomplishments and abilities, it is distressing that Carroll did not, particularly in the 1940s, achieve his potential. Curiously enough, his career in one basic respect parallels O'Casey's. They both successfully started with a gripping realistic play —*Things That Are Caesar's* and *The Shadow of a Gunman;* then they experienced two hit dramas, and then a decline from their two most important works. Unlike O'Casey, however, Carroll did not possess the lyrical and poetic qualities that would have given his secondary work more distinction. But, like O'Casey, he became caught up and waylaid by the siren call of symbolism and allegory and also, like O'Casey, he became too message-and-thesis conscious so that with the advent of *Kindred,* instead of the themes emerging subtly from the play, they too often seem to be the principal reason for the play's existence.

If Carroll is not so great a dramatist as he should have been, these are the reasons why. He came to allow his heart to rule his head, to preach almost unceasingly the nobleness of, and need for, love, dignity, tolerance, and understanding at the expense of retaining consistent dramatic control, clearness, and firmness. To say this, however, is not to ignore the fact that as long as the modern English theatre exists, Carroll's best dramas will be played, and these works, and the characters existing therein, are sufficient reason indeed for placing him in the pantheon of significant modern playwrights.

Selected Bibliography

There exists no complete bibliography of Paul Vincent Carroll's writings. Some of his plays exist only in typescript, although all but a few have been produced. Only a small number of his many short stories (he wrote over fifty stories for Scottish periodicals alone) have been collected. Most of the best studies of Carroll's plays have been written by Carroll himself in various articles appearing in the *New York Times*. The following bibliography of his dramas is actually the most complete presently available.

PLAYS

The Watched Pot (1930). Staged at the Peacock Theatre, Dublin. Unpublished.

Things That Are Caesar's. London: Rich and Cowan, Ltd., 1934.

Shadow and Substance. New York: Random House, 1937. London: Macmillan, 1938.

The White Steed and Coggerers (*Coggerers* is a one-act play, later retitled *Conspirators*) . New York: Random House, 1939.

Plays for My Children. New York: Julian Messner, 1939 (Contains "The King Who Could Not Laugh," "His Excellency—the Governor," "St. Francis and the Wolf,"

"Beauty is Fled," "Death Closes All," and "Maker of Roads"). Each of these one-act plays was published separately in 1947 by Samuel French, Ltd., London.

Kindred (1939). Produced in Dublin and New York. Unpublished. Revised form—*The Secret Kindred.* Unpublished.

The Old Foolishness. London: Samuel French, Ltd., 1944.

Three Plays: The White Steed, Things That Are Caesar's, The Strings, My Lord, Are False. London: Macmillan, 1944. The text of *Things That Are Caesar's* published in this volume is a revised version of the original play first performed in 1932 and first published in 1934.

Green Cars Go East. London: Samuel French, Ltd., 1947.

Interlude (a one-act play). London: Samuel French, Ltd., 1947.

Conspirators. London: Samuel French, Ltd., 1947.

The Wise Have Not Spoken. London: Samuel French, Ltd., 1947. New York: Dramatists Play Service, 1954.

Two Plays: The Wise Have Not Spoken—Shadow and Substance. London: Macmillan, 1948.

Weep for Tomorrow. London: M. Hemery, 1948 [a typescript]. A revised version of this play entitled *Goodbye to the Summer* (1956) has been published by Robert Hogan's Proscenium Press, Newark, Delaware, 1970.

Chuckeyhead Story. New York: Rialto Service Bureau, n.d. [a typescript]. The title of this play was changed to *Border Be Damned* (1951) and ultimately to *The Devil Came from Dublin* in 1951. Revisions were made in all three texts.

The Wayward Saint. New York: Dramatists Play Service, 1955.

Irish Stories and Plays. New York: Devin-Adair Co., 1958. (Contains the full length play *The Devil Came from Dublin,* three one-act plays—*The Conspirators, Beauty is Fled, Interlude*—and eight short stories.) This printed version of *The Devil Came from Dublin* is a revised form of the earlier play bearing the same title.

Farewell To Greatness. Dixon, California: Proscenium Press, 1966. Televised on B.B.C. in 1956 with Micheal MacLiammoir playing Swift. Not as yet produced on the stage.

Curtain Call, The Posthumous Papers of Paul Vincent Carroll. Robert Hogan is in the process of publishing (University of Missouri Press) several fugitive pieces by Carroll including two unpublished dramas—the full length play *We Have Ceased to Live* (never staged) and an unproduced television play about Robert Emmet, *The Darling of Erin.* (Carroll originally wrote a full length play about Emmet in the early 1930s, but this effort was never produced because, as Kavanagh observed in *The Story of the Abbey Theatre,* the characters did not take on vivid and life-like qualities.) Carroll turned some of this material into "Death Closes All," a children's play which was eventually published in 1939. The fast-paced, at times overly melodramatic, *Darling of Erin* is a much revised version of the original drama and the subsequent script of "Death Closes All." Professor Hogan's compilation also includes several essays (the majority of which have been published in the *New York Times* or in *Theatre Arts*), one unpublished short story, four poems, some letters, and a 1968 television interview conducted by John O'Donovan.

Proscenium Press hopes eventually to issue Carroll's unproduced and unpublished drama *Bitter Harvest,* an adaptation of Zola's *Thérèse Raquin.*

ARTICLES BY CARROLL

"The Substance of Paul Vincent Carroll," *New York Times,* January 30, 1938, Sect. 10, p. 1.

"Irish Eyes Are Smiling," *New York Times,* April 17, 1938, Sect. 10, pp. 1–2.

"On Legend and the Arts," *New York Times,* January 8, 1939, Sect. 9, p. 3.

"Scotland's Dramatic Genius is Flowering," *Theatre Arts,* XXIX (May 1945), 283–286.

"The Irish Theatre (Post-war)," *International Theatre,* ed. John Andrews and Ossia Trilling. London: Sampson Low, 1949, pp. 122–128.

"Can the Abbey Theatre Be Restored?" *Theatre Arts,* XXXVI (January 1952), 18–19, 79.

"The Mystical Irish," *The Vanishing Irish,* ed. John A. O'Brien. New York: McGraw-Hill, 1953, pp. 60–70.

"Reforming a Reformer," *New York Times,* February 13, 1955, Sect. 2, pp. 1, 3.

"The Rebel Mind," *New York Times,* January 24, 1960, Sect. 2, p. 3.

ARTICLES ABOUT CARROLL

John Mason Brown, "Cathleen ni Houlihan and *Shadow and Substance,*" *Two on the Aisle: Ten Years of the American Theatre in Performance.* New York: Norton, 1938, pp. 130–132.

John Mason Brown, "Ireland and *The White Steed,*" *Broadway in Review.* New York: Norton, 1940, pp. 205–208.

Sr. Anne G. Coleman, "Paul Vincent Carroll's View of Irish Life," *Catholic World,* CXCII (November 1960), 87–93.

Robert Hogan, "Paul Vincent Carroll: The Rebel as Prodigal Son," *After the Irish Renaissance.* Minneapolis: University of Minnesota Press, 1967.

Micheal MacLiammoir, "Problem Plays," *The Irish Theatre,* ed. Lennox Robinson. London: Macmillan, 1939, pp. 200–227.

George Jean Nathan, "The Devil Came from Dublin," *Theatre Arts,* XXXV (November 1951), 66–67.

Drew B. Pallette, "Paul Vincent Carroll—Since *The White Steed," Modern Drama,* VII (February 1965) , 375–381.

Hugh Smith, "Irish Dramatist Objects," *New York Times,* July 30, 1939, Sect. 9, p. 2.

Hugh Smith, "Mr. Carroll's 'Kindred,' " *New York Times,* October 8, 1939, Sect. 9, p. 3.